ACBN

Afrikan-Centered Biological Nationalism

A Primer

Copyright Page

First Edition
First Printing: 2017
ISBN: 978-0-578-19540-7
First eBook Version: 2017

Son of Ahset Publications
East Afrikan Community - Burundi- Kenya - Tanzania - Rwanda - Uganda

www.sonofahset.wordpress.com

Cover art by *SunMyke*

Includes bibliographic references

For Myra and Bronson

Table of Contents

Acknowledgments

I would like to dedicate this text to the work and legacy of Dr. Amos N. Wilson. Dr. Wilson's impact on Afrikan philosophical thought is virtually unequalled in the latter part of the 20th century. At my first occasion to hear him speak via recorded video in 2010, I thought his analysis of the psychological basis of the socio-economic and political condition in which Afrikans find ourselves was unparalleled and refreshingly honest. I particularly remember the moment when I heard him charge the USA with being a "crimogenic" society, that is a society that literally produces criminality as a result of its socio-political system, and is the USA's reason for being now. At that moment, I decided that this was the man with whom I had to work for the reminder of my productive years—at whatever project he happened to be involved with at the time. So, I did an internet search to find his whereabouts and discovered that he had already died in 1994. I sat there astonished. I could not reconcile the fact that Dr. Wilson had existed during a time when I was alive and I had no knowledge of his existence. I plainly could not fathom how a man like this could barely be known, considering the myriad of talk shows and political interest programming that abounds now and then. It was literally disconcerting for me to think that this man was not more prominent in the public consciousness during his most productive years. However, I suspected that the usual characters who promote integration, multiculturalism, Americanism, and "individual striving" as an action plan for Black people did know of his existence, both then and now. This meant that they willingly and knowingly marginalized a man whose work and intellect could have had a decisive change on the perceptions of Afrikan youth both in the USA, the Afrikan continent, and other Afrikan diasporic populations. The effort to keep him hidden from the mass populous was tantamount to criminality, just as Dr. Wilson had ascertained. This book is dedicated to the tremendous analysis and intellectual heft he brought to studying the Afrikan situation in the world and the efforts we must make to steer our Afrikans societies toward power.

I would also like to acknowledge other authors who have influenced this work due to their dedication to providing a significant contribution to the canon of Afrikan philosophical-political thought. They are Marcus Garvey, (The Philosophy and Opinions of Marcus Garvey) Dr. Marimba Ani (Yurugu & Let the Circle Be Unbroken), Mwalimu K. Bomani Baruti (Homosexuality and the Effeminization of Afrikan Males), and Dr. Chancellor Williams (The Destruction of Afrikan Civilization). There are of course more authors and thinkers who have influenced me and the creation of this work, but the aforementioned are the most notable and lay the foundation for understanding all other relevant works about the Afrikan condition.

Two other writers I would be remiss in not mentioning who have also written books related to this subject are Trojan Pam and Rashida Strober. Trojan Pam has written a remarkable series of books on subjects ranging from false beauty standards and interracial relationships, to Black relationships and the national oppression of Black people under domination by whites and other groups. Rashida Strober, *"The World's Frist Dark Skin Activist"* has made it her personal mission to bring the issue she refers to as *"Darkism"* to the public consciousness in which she correctly charges non-Black people (and some Black people) for harboring an aversion to people with noticeable and unmistakably dark skin. She has written a number of books and plays on this subject and in my opinion, is on the right track towards providing literature and artworks to address the psychological issues of being Black in a world which has been taught to prefer pale-skinned people. Their works can be found at the following websites:

Trojan Pam: racismws.com
Rashida Strober: darkiskinisbeautifulcampaign.com

Next, I want to thank three people who really brought the issue of this book to the forefront of my mind. The first person is a content creator who operated under the moniker *"Moving Africa 2 Freedom"*. He was the first person who really started examining this issue of African identity with regard to biology that I had ever encountered. His commitment to the honest discussion of the subject was commendable, and I thank him very much for that. Two other gentleman who similarly examined this issue and wrote hundreds of articles examining current events from this perspective are the authors of two informative and cutting-edge websites. One writes at acbnj.wordpress.com and goes by the name Bhekizitha. He has been resolute in keeping this issue in the public sphere. The other gentleman is named Gaspar Yanga, and also writes under the "jina la kalamu" (pen name) *Amos Wilson University*. His online magazine is called *Amos Magazine* and can also be found at the wordpress site. These two Afrikan men have been admirable in their steadfastness to discuss this issue as one of the central hurdles to acquiring the modicum of focus which is required to secure power and psychological self-respect for Afrikan people. I thank both of them for their noteworthy influence on this book.

Finally, special thanks go to the Afrikan ancestors whose spirit and wisdom guided the writing of this book. Duau emakyu, duau ntru, duau!

Introduction

Primer - *n* /prim-er/ 1. An elementary book for teaching children to read. 2. **any book of elementary principles**

According the above definition, a book which espouses basic principles and/or ideas with the purpose to teach is called *a primer*. That is what this book is. It is by no means a comprehensive treatise on political philosophy or an in-depth survey of the various topics which are discussed herein. It is quite simply an argument for the basic rationale behind Afrikan-Centered Biological Nationalism (ACBN) and a basis for social reconstruction among Black people. The necessary social reconstruction I argue will then provide the foundation for first cultural, then economic, and ultimately political-military regeneration of Afrikan people as a globally recognized people-force with the power to support, develop, protect, and if necessary, impose its distinctive worldview. The aim of this activity is to ensure the biological survival of actual Afrikan people.

The direction this book will take will include a discussion on a few pertinent topics which intersect with the political philosophy of ACBN. The main topic is defining biologically who is an Afrikan in the most simplistic terms possible. It is the view of the author that Afrikans have not yet asserted the right to create definitions and enforce them through powerful and institutional means. This is a main element in why we face derision and scorn throughout the world as a group. We have accepted both magnanimous and pejorative definitions created by others which may or may not be accurate in the hopes of benefitting by emulating these foreign concepts. We do so because we feel if we prostrate ourselves before our enemies, we will suffer less and might survive a little while longer, and even prosper individually.

I will discuss interracial relationships (IR) and how they damage the definition of who is an Afrikan. I will discuss the social cohesion which is adversely affected by the proliferation and condoning of these arrangements, particularly by Afrikan people. I attempt to explain in the best way I can the psycho-social and political reasons why both Afrikan people choose non-Afrikan mates and why non-Afrikan people choose Afrikan mates. I will show that despite the proliferation of images and examples of IR relationships in the media, most non-Afrikan groups actually mate and marry within their own racial group. The only exception to this behavior is within the Afrikan group where the largest percentage of males in all racial groups who in fact mate/marry interracially are Afrikan males. Conversely, the woman least likely to mate/marry interracially is an Afrikan female. In addition, an anecdotal overview of the hybrid offspring of these sexual unions will be discussed as well in an attempt to dispel the myth that no one is adversely affected by an interracial couple's decision to mate and breed mixed-race kids.

I will include a discussion on the necessity of at least one Afrikan national group within the larger Afrikan biological group developing a sociopolitical theory. I will attempt to relate the creation of this theory to the cultural, economic, and political development of power for the biological Afrikan group globally which would extend to every biological Afrikan person wherever they are in the world. A strategy will be proposed for how to begin to implement such a theory on the individual level and by doing so create the momentum to impact institutions with the ACBN approach. The institutional inertia which will be developed should have a residual effect far into the future if committed people accept the task and mission at hand.

I also discuss where the best location is for operating and developing this power that Afrikans need. I specifically focus on America, but it can be a stand-in for any European expatriate colonial state or metropole such as Canada, Brazil, the Caribbean islands, the UK, or France. I compare America with a short examination of Afrika as a locale to establish this geopolitical footing.

Finally, I give some concluding thoughts and suggest some solutions for the dilemma that Afrikan people currently face. The purpose of the book is to give Afrikan individuals who are concerned with: (1) *the development of power for Afrikans*, (2) *the survival of authentic*

Afrikan people, and (3) *the promotion and persistence of the authentic, archetypical Afrikan as the exemplar of our race*, a handbook to understand an approach to the eventual reclamation of Afrikan sovereignty that has not as yet been tried. I do not write an objective book. Throughout the book, I will disclose my particular biases unashamedly, so as to provide the reader with as much of my personal point of view as possible. For example, I reject and <u>do not</u> believe that we need all (or even most) Afrikans to be in agreement about a socio-political program in order to initiate one. I <u>do not</u> think that we need all Afrikan nations in alignment with one unitary policy of achieving power in the world. Lastly, I <u>do not</u> think all Afrikan people can or need to be "saved" (whatever that means). I wholeheartedly understand the concept and reality of **the traitor** and do not think that just because someone is Afrikan that they need to be recruited to our cause or will be an asset to it. In view of statements like the aforementioned, I compel the reader to evaluate and research the veracity of other statements I will make so as to ascertain their viability. I am not opposed to correction where necessary to clarify my essential proposition. However, I am not interested in vitriolic detractors who disagree with my position in order to push their contradictory positions. If an error is cited to exist in this book, and that error is used to support a contradictory position, that is not a use which I envision for this polemic. I maintain my propagation of *Afrikan-Centered Biological Nationalism/**ACBN*** as the only socio-political theory that will lay the proper basis for the functional survival for Afrikan people on this planet.

Chapter 1: Who is an Afrikan?

Definition

"An Afrikan person is a person within the skin color range of brown to black with Afrikan textured hair" ~Bhekizitha[1]

I use the above definition as my basic definition of an Afrikan person. However, to be more precise, I use the following definition to provide more details.

First of all, I want to state for the purposes here that "Black" (person) and "Afrikan" are synonyms. I would also say that an Afrikan person is someone with two Afrikan parents. Thus, an Afrikan is a man, woman, or child (boy or girl) that has intense, rich, and profuse epidermal melanin content which results in a bold and conspicuous dark brown to deeply brown skin color. Additionally, an Afrikan man, woman, boy, or girl has coarsely textured hair that in its natural state and without chemical application is elliptical and tightly spiraled. The hair is resistant to making substantial motion from a static position due to a light wind or sudden neck movements, or other light physical contact. It is not straight, wavy, or curly and the hair (or short locks) do not fall limply towards the body, but the hair naturally grows up and outward from the head unless the hair is braided or locked.

When discussing important issues with people, some have the tendency to focus on meaningless details in an effort to stall the conversation at an inconsequential point of disagreement so that the full implications of the conclusion will never be reached, and thus action cannot be undertaken. So even though the definition quoted from Bhekizitha is an apt one, with which I wholly agree, I felt the need to provide within the elaborated definition a description of what an Afrikan person is not. My definition is biological and not geographical. So, an Afrikan person is not a person who was simply born on the Afrikan continent. However, the biological group to which I am referring is largely concentrated on the Afrikan continent hence the land mass is used to refer to the people as well, not invaders or settlers whose origin is elsewhere. Therefore, since a white person

1

living in Korea will never be Korean, no matter how long he or she is there, and regardless of whether or not they have white children in that country, they are not Korean, and never will be. An Afrikan is not every member of the homo sapien sapiens population on earth. An Afrikan is not someone who has a hybrid parent, nor someone who is hybridized and simply identifies as Afrikan or with Afrikans. This is an important detail because I have personally seen many so-called Black activists, Afrocentric or "Pro-Black" people who talk the talk, but they mate with or marry a hybrid or very light-skinned, non-white man or woman. Others often excuse this by saying that there are "light-skinned, Black people" (a contradiction in terms) because of "slave rape". So, this means due to the historical fact that white men raped Afrikan women and produced hybrid kids, and even that some white women had illicit and exploitative affairs with Afrikan men during enslavement and possibly did the same, therefore everyone who is a "light-skinned, Black person" today, is here due to this activity. This argument commits the logical fallacy of *affirming the consequent*. Meaning that the argument is invalid because condition 3 is not necessarily caused by condition 1 and 2, even if condition one and two are true. In other words, the following logical fallacy is employed by those who attribute slave rape to the modern presence of so-called "light-skinned, Black people".

[Condition 1] White men raped and impregnated Afrikan woman during slavery.

[Condition 2] "Light-skinned, Black people" have some Afrikan ancestry.

[Condition 3] Therefore, "light-skinned, Black people" are products of slave rape.

It is obvious to me that this line of argumentation is employed for emotional reasons naturally connected to the horror and criminality of white men raping Afrikan women with Afrikan men having little to no power to stop it or seek retribution. It is also used to justify the choice of a non-Afrikan mate some Black men make to shame other Afrikan people into accepting the wife or children as fully Black.

So, in addition to this, I would say, notwithstanding all the great political analysis and good he might have done, that Malcom X is not an Afrikan either because his mother was a mulatto. This will serve as a shock and wake-up call to these people who think that they can talk "bad Black talk" and then turn around and run to marry the lightest person they can find and have children with them. If Malcolm X is seen as a non-Afrikan/non-white asset to the Afrikan project for sovereign power, then it serves as a notice to everyone that we will not recognize offspring of an Afrikan and a mulatto as an Afrikan, much less an Afrikan and a non-Afrikan. So, people really should consider deeply the choice they make in a mate and try one's level best to indeed "help who they fall in love with" and not to let things "just happen".

Evidence of Afrikans through population data of the continent

Some people would refute the above definition for various reasons. One such reason is that white Arabs, Europeans and others have been on the continent for hundreds of years and some have made contributions to Afrikans or helped Afrikans in some way, so now they should be seen as Afrikan too. I must state the following definitively. Being Afrikan is not a reward one gets for longevity and distinguished service. It is not like getting a wristwatch at retirement or something. At its core being Afrikan is biological and is handed down genetically via one's direct ancestors. I have had a Tanzanian-Afrikan person tell me that America became a great nation because it has a diverse population, and so for Afrikan nations to develop, they should become inclusive and diverse as well. One Ghanaian-Afrikan told me that the first-generation Lebanese man living in Ghana, merely one generation removed from immigration mind you (after the decolonization period in the fifties), who now owns a Ghanaian football club, is in fact a Ghanaian now. This is because he wears

Ghanaian fashion and makes a spectacle of himself by being seen on TV cheering loudly for the team when they score goals. Another Afrikan female told me, when I challenged her after she taught a classroom full of young Afrikan girls that _fair-skinned is more beautiful_, that "all Tanzanians are not Black". This was in reference to a white, east Indian woman who apparently had won the Miss Tanzania beauty contest some years ago[2]. We have the so-called issue of "Colorism" (which I will address more fully later) which charged actual Black people in the USA for practicing such when they correctly pointed out that the winner of the Miss Black University of Texas pageant was in fact not Black at all[3]. She was a multi-racial person who did not even have at least one Black parent. I say all of this to state that with so much confusion about who is actually Afrikan, a practical definition is sorely needed. Not the least of which is for our rational sociopolitical-economic development. We need to know definitively who is in the group and who is not.

The concept of multiculturalism has further sullied the understanding of who is in fact an Afrikan. People think that in the era of _passport nationalism_ that simply carrying the official paperwork of a predefined geo-political zone makes one the member of a distinctive biological group. However, upon closer examination, one will see that the "multiculturalism" which is touted to exist in some Afrikan and Caribbean nations are but a mere illusion put forward by a global media infrastructure with an agenda to foster confusion and force people to accept erroneous views of reality. The population of Afrikan people in the vast majority of non-Arab strongholds in Afrika are overwhelmingly Afrikan. When I say non-Arab, I do not mean non-Muslim. I am talking about areas where white Arabs conquered during the initial phase of the militant spread of Islam. This is limited to North Afrika and some areas of East Afrika. The specific countries include Algeria, Morocco, Mauritania, Tunisia, Libya, Egypt, Western Sahara, and Sudan (however, Sudan is a multi-racial society with plenty of actual Afrikans living there, as is Ethiopia).

I must also expound on the prior parenthetical statement. Some dark-skinned people living in Afrikan nations are not actually bio-

4

genetically Afrikan. This can be seen when examining the hair which a preponderance of them have. It is not Afrikan-textured hair according to the definition. This is due to historical mixing with Arabs and other migrants which changed the genotype in that region into what we see manifested in the phenotype today. People assume that because someone lives in Ethiopia, Somalia, Eritrea, Djibouti or Sudan that they are automatically Afrikan because they have dark skin. This is not true. These areas are clinal zones. Clinal zones are geographical areas where two biogenetically different people met and engaged in massive intermarrying and interbreeding. The result is that the offspring resembles neither of the two biogenetic parental groups completely. This can be seen in the resultant wider skin color range and lack of Afrikan-textured hair among the people in this area. I will add a caveat that this does not include ALL people in these clinal zones. There are a large and significant population of authentic Afrikan people in these areas, but due to economic and cultural colonization, together with a distorted view from the media, we do not actually see these Afrikans either in pictures or in the major metropolitan areas very often. A trip beyond the major cities would reveal a stark difference between the Ethiopian or Somali that we typically see in the media, and the distinctive features of the Afrikans located in other towns and rural areas. Being located along the nautical trade routes provided access to many merchants and migrants to seek refuge and markets in these zones[4]. So, for whatever reason, the outcome was the mixed-race, non-Afrikan hybrids populating the trade routes and metropoles. The Afrikans who were disinterested (for whatever reason) in interbreeding, maintained themselves in the inland and other areas.

Consider the following quote:

> *"I would never want to belong to a club that would have someone like me for a member."*

~Woody Allen (quoting Groucho Marx)[5]

The above quote, although attributed to two different Jews, typifies the behavior some authentic Afrikans exhibit when faced with the reality of their distinct biological traits. Afrikans recoil at the thought of being an exclusive group as if it diminishes us personally in some way if we are "forced" to be grouped with other Black people. Some Afrikans furiously try to include other non-Afrikans, ofttimes against their will, because many of us just can't stand the thought of existing as a stand-alone population. People quickly retort, *"Well it's a globalized world now!"* As if this dispels the need for definition, internal organizations, boundaries, and standards. What people really mean is that they want to be with non-Afrikan people, so in a roundabout way they are saying, *"I don't wanna hear any of that Black stuff."*

In order to provide some evidence, I included the following table to show ethnographic information for the region of the Afrikan continent where authentic Afrikans predominate. The Arab colonies of the north (except Mauritania) and the clinal zones are not included due to the likelihood of a discrepancy in how the data were collected concerning the definition of who is Black, who is mixed, and who is an Arab. As we will see later, some Afrikans identify as "Arab" because they have adopted the foreign religion of Islam. If the term "Black", "Black African", or an ethnic group designation was used, I included it to show that the vast majority of people in these areas are still listed as Black, and only an insignificant minority (except in the case of South Africa and some islands in the Caribbean) are other than Black/Afrikan. Mauritania was included to show that the legacy of white Arab enslavement of Afrikans still exists.

Table 1. Racial Data of a Sample of Supra-Saharan[6] Afrikan Countries

Afrikan Nation	Afrikan population*	Non-Afrikan population	Unspecified (data also listed as *other*)
Angola	75%	2% mestico/hybrid 1% European	22% Other
oBahamas	90%	4.7% white 2.1% mixed	1.9% Other 0.7 Unspec
Benin	97%	1.9% foreigner	0.9%
Botswana	93%	7%**	
Burkina Fasso	92.9%		7.1% Unspec
Burundi	99%	3000 Europeans 2000 S. Asians	
Cameroon	99%	1%	
Republic of Congo	97%	3% European and other	
Ivory Coast	74.8%		25.2 Unspec
Ghana	98.4		1.4 Other
Kenya	99%	1% European, Asian, Arab	
Mozambique	99.66%	0.2% Mixed 0.06% European 0.08 Indians	
Mauritania	**70%**	**30% Arab**	
Namibia	87.5%	6.5% mixed 6% White	
Niger	98.9	0.4 Arab	0.9% Other
Nigeria	100%		
Rwanda	100%		
Senegal	90.7%	9.3% European and Lebanese	
oSt. Lucia	85.3%	10.9% mixed 2.2% E. Indian	1.7% Other/Unspec
oSt. Vincent/ Grenadines	66%	19% Mixed 6% E. Indian 4% European 2% Carib Amerindian	3% Other
South Sudan	100%		
South Afrika	80.2%	8.4% European 8.8% Colored (mixed) 2.5% Indian/Asian	
Tanzania	99%	1% mixed, Arab, European, Indian	
Zimbabwe	99.4%		0.6% Other/Unspec

*Afrikan population includes all indigenous, sub-national ethnicities.
**Some population in the unspecified/other category may be Afrikan, so the percentage of Afrikans might be higher in each region.
***Includes Kgalagadi and White populations.
o Nations with Afrikan populations due to being captured and enslaved during *The Black Chattelization War* 1442-1888

As we saw in the chart, Mauritania still has a majority Afrikan population despite being dominated and enslaved by Arabs to this day.[7] So, Afrikans still need to be organized even if we are in the majority. Attempting to breed whites out or to create a permanent white minority due to the majority of "people of color" existing in a region, does not necessarily produce power for the majority group. There are several other factors which must be present to assure political control. In addition, two more interesting cases which highlight the need for ACBN and its basis in the definition of who is an Afrikan are the following countries of Cape Verde and Chad. We can see in the data the clear reality of the different biogenetic categorization of hybrids when they are in the majority. Also, we see the confusion of Afrikans who have accepted a foreign ideology to their own detriment and to the disadvantage of the Afrikan group as a whole in the case of Chad.

Table 2. Racial Data of Cape Verde Population

Afrikan Nation	Afrikan population*	Non-Afrikan population
Cape Verde	28%	71% Creole (mulatto) 1% European

Table 3. Racial Data of Chad Population

Afrikan Nation	Afrikan population*	Non-Afrikan population	Unspecified (data also listed as other)
Chad	87.3%	9.6% Arabs	3.0% Other/Unspec

Even though the overwhelming majority of Chadian-Afrikans are indigenous, with only a population slightly under 10% of Arabs, the people who claim Islam as their religion totals 53.1%[8] of the population. Therefore, we cannot know for sure from the data if any people identifying as Arabs are in fact Afrikans wishing to escape their biogenetic group to be closer to Allah. This also implies an Arab stronghold on some sectors of the economy. I seriously doubt Arabs have migrated to Chad to be second or third-class citizens marginally surviving under Afrikan domination. The main problem is the projected population growth of Chad[9] which given the less that ideal performance of the economic conditions, insinuates that a large exodus of Chadian-Afrikans might occur in the coming years to parts other that Afrika. Infused with a foreign ideology and desperate for economic opportunity, this development might not bode well for the ability of Afrikans to organize for effective power systems. Afrikan groups like the Chadian-Afrikans could fall prey to influence from Muslim Arabs, or other ideologies to work against the interests of Afrikans, if we fail to recognize the dire need for a cohering framework for organizing Afrikans now.

And for those of you running off to Belize because it is a "Black" country, please inspect the following ethnographic population data. It might prepare you for what you will actually see when you arrive there.

Table 4. Racial Data of Belize Population[†]

Afrikan Nation	Afrikan population*	Non-Afrikan population	Unspecified (data also listed as *other*)
Belize	6.1 % Garifuna	52.9% Mestizo 25.9% Creole 11.3% Maya 3.9% E. Indian 3.6% Mennonite 1.2% White 1% Asian	1.2% Other 0.3% Unknown

[†]Percentages add up to more than 100% because respondents were able to identify more than one ethnic origin. (2010 est.)

Here is another example which is quite interesting. It seems Afrikans and Indians are having quite an island party without inviting *us*! Either that, or they are getting a jump start on that "raceless" society which will be coming any day now.

Table 5. Racial Data of Trinidad & Tobago

Afrikan Nation	Afrikan population*	Non-Afrikan population	Unspecified (data also listed as other)
Trinidad & Tobago	34.2%	35.4% Indian 15.3% mixed-other 7.7% mixed Indian-Afrikan	7.5% Other/Unspec

It can be clearly seen from these population data that the classification of multiracial hybrids comports not only to their own innate sense and biogenetic fact of identity, but it has political consequences as well, particularly in the case of Cape Verde where they dominate the population _and_ government. Europeans have conveniently categorized non-white groups according to their own political needs. Through Europeans' clever use of the _rhetorical ethic_ (more on that later), they have us believing that hybrids, mulattos, bi-racial, multiracial people, mixed-race people (whatever you want to call them) can all be Afrikan too. This is particularly practiced in the areas of the world where Europeans are undisputedly politically dominant like the USA and the UK.

How Afrikans looked from time immemorial

If people look at the photographic evidence of Afrikan people taken after the invention of the camera in the 19th century, we can see physical evidence of the physical traits which Afrikan people have. We can also look at sketches, drawings and other renderings from the pre-photographic period to come to the same conclusion. Although it is obvious that mulattos and other mixed-race individuals existed in these eras, there existence is not documented in the same manner as are the Afrikans whom the Europeans and Arabs were enslaving and shipping to various parts of the world. Since having the traits of an Afrikan conferred the lowest status on a human being at that time and now, we can be reasonably confident that the phenotype displayed in the pictorial evidence is consistent with how Afrikans looked both upon European and Arab arrival, and from time immemorial. Let's look at some evidence of Afrikans and compare it to pictures in which it can be definitively seen or is stated that the person is a mulatto or mixed-race.

In these two renderings depicting activity on the coffle lines (above) and on an enslaver's ship (below), we can see that the artist drew the Afrikans with uniformity of appearance in hair, skin color, and physical build. This indicates that this is how Afrikans appeared to the Europeans both in Afrika and in the colonial west, where these drawings were made.

Here is a photograph which also depicts Afrikans as showing uniformity in appearance with respect to hair and skin color. They are certainly distinct from the Europeans who make up the crew of enslavers on the HMS Daphne (1866-1879). This ship is embarking from East Afrika.

Here is another rendering which depicts Afrikans and the Arab enslavers. It too shows distinctive difference between the paler Arabs and darker Afrikans. The Afrikans also have a general uniformity of appearance and do not show disparate skin tones nor hair textures.

This photo from the 1890s depicts Afrikans kidnapped to be sold in the Arab slave trade in East Afrika also. Again, notice the general uniformity of appearance in skin color, hair, and physical build.

In this photograph from the 19th century, we see Afrikans showing the same uniformity of appearance in hair, skin color, and physical build which are again distinct from the paler Arabs enslavers in the left side of the photo. This photo is also from the Eastern Afrikan, Arab enslavement activity.

Somali-Afrikan woman referred to as a Bantu who was enslaved by white Arabs in Mogadishu (1882-1883). Notice the quintessential Afrikan features in her face and skin color which are unmistakably associated with Afrikans. She is quite different from the curly-haired Somalis which are often seen immigrating to the west and depicted in news media videos and pictures. She is indistinct from Afrikans encountered in Western, Central, and Southern Afrika.

Somali woman with obvious genetic admixture. She now identifies as a "Somali-American and was elected to a legislative body in the USA. She is quite distinct from the previous picture and has no obvious Afrikan physical features.

Somali President Hassan Sheikh Mohamud. His hair is not Afrikan-textured even though he is within the color range of Afrikans. This indicates he is a product of genetic admixture from previous generations of Arab or Asiatic invaders. The wider color range and differing physical features of the two people in the photos is a result of such historical genetic infusion.

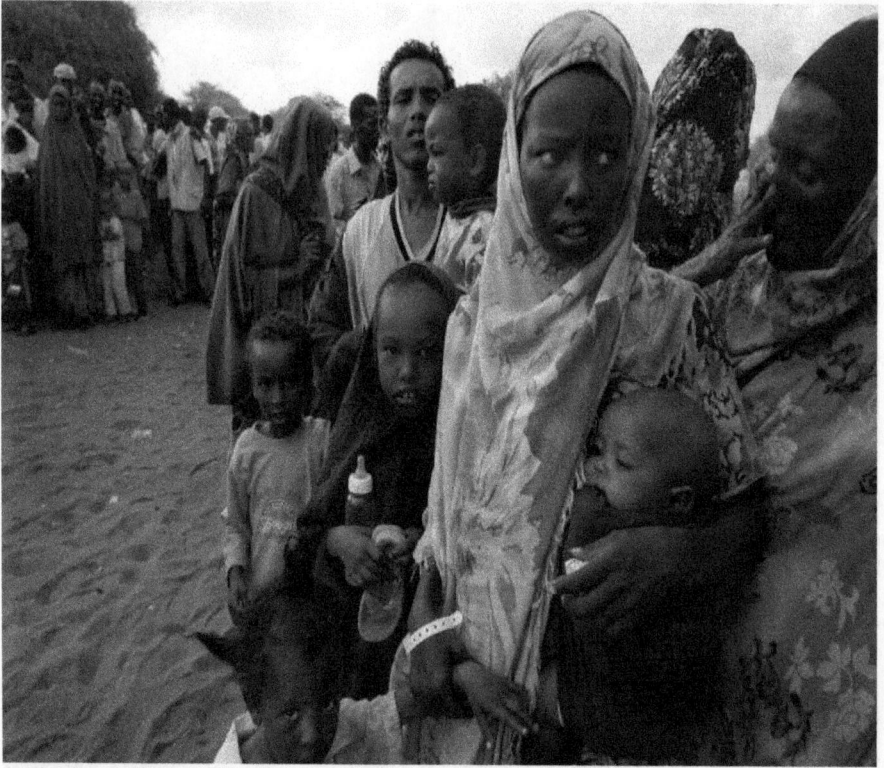

Present day Somalis, some of whom have obvious Afrikan physical features and some have non-Afrikan physical features. Some have non-Afrikan textured hair and some do not. The women may have Afrikan-textured hair, but we can't know for sure due to the head garment they are wearing. However, their faces are distinctly Afrikan as opposed to the man and boy standing behind them. He is distinct from the men in the background of the picture who are closer in appearance to the Afrikan women in the foreground. This picture is representative of the Sahel and Horn regions of African who have genetic admixture from Arab and Asiatic invasions going back a couple of millennia.

The above photo is an Ethiopian woman with obvious non-Afrikan features. She is both outside of the color range and does not have Afrikan-textured hair. Incidentally, she identifies as "Jewish" and desires to live among her people, the European Jews in Israel. What if she marries a European Jew and brings him to Afrika claiming he is Afrikan too because he is a Jew and has a "Jewish-Afrikan" wife? This is how multiculturalism is actually anti-Afrikan and dangerous. It would be easy for this Jewish man to buy up Afrikan resources with loans from his Jewish cousins and isolate Afrikans from our own wealth. Multiculturalism does not work for Afrikan people.

Ethiopian man Tedros Adhanom Ghebreyesus. He is an official at the United Nations and serves as the WHO Director General. News reports stated that he was the "first African" to hold this position.

17

Photgraph of enslaved Afrikan women and children—19th century in the Americas. Notice the similarity of appearance in hair and skin color.

"A group of men and boys at the dock in Jacksonville, Florida, in the mid-19th century. The slave trade was in the process of being stamped out by then. Courts were set up to adjudicate captured slave ships leading to the raft of documents available today." (Again, uniformity of appearance.)

Photograph taken of Afrikan girl in the Americas in the 19th century.

African woman in the Americas photographed from the 19th century.

"April 1865; Alexander Gardner, photographer. Shows group of five African America females (perhaps four women and a girl) and a boy on an island in the James River." (See Photo Credits)

As can be seen in the photo, all of the people have clear Afrikan looks and a similar appearance in skin color and facial features, except the white boy in the foreground.

Afrikan woman in the USA or Brazil photographed in the 19th century.

(Don't ever forget how these people forced our women to care for their kids while neglecting our own, Black man! After all, who really were the lazy ones?)

"Studio portrait of 'African American' woman in long formal and feather fan hat; circa late 19th century/early 20th century; by Norman Studios in Natchez, Mississippi." [Quotation marks mine]

It is obvious that this woman is a mulatto or mixed-race when compared to the other pictures I showed previously. However, she is incorrectly referred to as "African American" which implies that one is "Black/Afrikan" without specifically referring to her European family members.

Recently "discovered" by Henry Louis Gates is this woman, Sarah Farro. She is referred to as a "Black" novelist when she is obviously of mixed-race as well. Notice the different texture of hair and the skin color which is outside of the range of Afrikans. This woman lived and wrote in Britain, so it is very likely that she was a mulatto. This photo is from the late 19th century, probably 1880s or 1890s.

"Studio portrait of African American young girl; circa late 19th century/early 20th century; by Norman Studios in Natchez, Mississippi".

Again, it is wrongly stated that this girl is African American, a phrase which has no clear definition. Is it a person with mixed ancestry? Is it a person with one American (European) parent and one Afrikan parent? Is it a Black/Afrikan person only? What does it mean? This girl is clearly a mulatto, but again she would be incorrectly given the designation as "Black" and thereby absolving her white family members (and nation) of any claim or responsibility over her. Like the earlier depiction on page 24, we Afrikans are still expected to provide childcare for the offspring of whites.

"Studio portrait of 'African American' young girl standing and holding a fan; circa late 19th century/early 20th century; by Norman Studios in Natchez, Mississippi"

I think my point has been made with the term *African American*. It is obvious that her hair is not Afrikan-textured hair, and her features are much more aquiline which indicates she has recent non-Afrikan heritage. She appears to look like some east Indians who have similar dark skin, but lanky hair. This is most likely due to mutation through sexually interbreeding and not the environmental conditions.

Daniel Payne in a photograph dated 1888. Notice his different skin color and hair texture. He was 'born free', meaning he was not a slave from birth. He was bishop, educator, college administrator and author. A major shaper of the A.M.E. church and co-founder of Wilberforce University. According to *Wikipedia*, Payne was "of African, European and Native American descent. Daniel stated, 'as far as memory serves me my mother was of light-brown complexion, of middle stature and delicate frame. She told me that her grandmother was of the tribe of Indians known in the early history of the Carolinas as the Catawba Indians.' He also stated that he descended from the Goings family, who were a well-known free colored/Native American family. His father was one of six brothers who served in the Revolutionary War and his paternal grandfather was an Englishmen. His parents London and Martha Payne were part of the "Brown Elite" of free "blacks" [Quotation marks mine] in the city."

So, we can see here a clear instance (in a long line of examples) of a multiracial, non-Afrikan person being called "Black"/ "African-American" and placed in leadership over Afrikan people. How can a non-Afrikan know what is in the best interests of Afrikan people? Especially when they do not even fully identify with us, and specifically go out of their way to identify with our enemies and others.

Here is another mulatto by the name of William Wells Brown. He is erroneously called the first "African-American" novelist, much like the mulatto Barack Obama is falsely called the first "Black" president in the USA (if you don't count Bill Clinton—thanks for nothing Toni Morrison!). He was a contemporary of Frederick Douglass. Brown specifically wrote books about mulattos as they were whom he identified with most. His book "Clotel: or The President's Daughter, A Narrative of Slave Life in the United States" was first published in 1853. It was subsequently published under various titles such as, "The Beautiful Quadroon", "A Romance of American Slavery", and "The Colored Heroine". The novel is loosely based on Thomas Jefferson and his mulatto mistress Sally Hemmings.

It is obvious from the picture that he does not fall within the skin color range of Afrikan people and he does not have Afrikan-textured hair. He resembles nothing of the Afrikans we saw in the previous photographs and actually looks more European that Afrikan to the eyes of this author.

Frederick Douglass, a well-known mulatto rabble-rouser like Colin Kaepernick or Jesse Williams. His history is readily available, so there is no need to expound on it here. I just want to point out that he does not have Afrikan-textured hair and despite the darkened image, his skin color was just at the border of what most Afrikan people have. This indicates that non-Afrikan, multiracial people can possess *some* of the traits of an Afrikan person, but to satisfy the biological definition, one must have <u>ALL</u> of the traits. Particularly, if it is known that one has a non-Afrikan parent like Frederick Douglass did. Besides, just on a side note, he always looked a little like Terence Trent D'arby to this author, who himself was a pop singer in the USA from the 1980s and was another known mulatto.

Here is a typical negro fighting in service of his white masters (France) during World War I to defeat a political foe of one faction of whites for another (Germany). He sees no need to fight for his own power in the world. The reward for his loyal service is the opportunity to breed himself out of existence and sully the genetics of the defeated European group, whom he never actually directly attacks. After he has satisfied himself with his war booty, he returns to where the whites who brought him in the first place to Germany really wanted him…which is back in "French" Colonial Africa or the other French colonies. This photograph, dated 1919, was used as propaganda to lure more Afrikan men into the French Colonial military service.

The product of such dangerous liaisons as depicted in the previous picture during the first half of *The European Imperialist 30 Years' War* (World War I). "*'Rhineland Bastard'*" was the term used in Nazi Germany to describe kids of mixed German and African parentage, who were fathered by Africans serving as French colonial troops occupying the Rhineland after World War I. Under National Socialism (Nazism) these kids were consigned to compulsory sterilization.

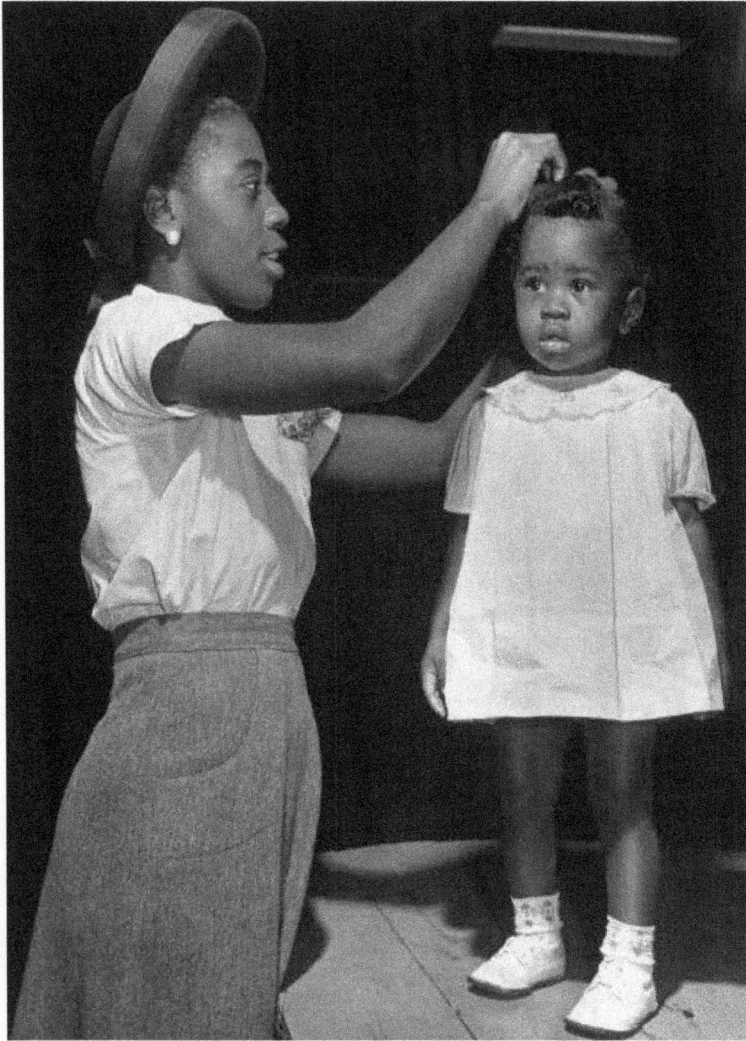

The true evidence and legacy of the existence of Afrikan men and Afrikan women is the Afrikan child. There is no taint of the misguided and lascivious behavior of wayward sexual interactions when a lovely mother and beautiful child exist to carry on your legacy Black man!

I purposefully saved this picture for last because the story is so outrageous that it drives home the point I am making with this photographic evidence. "The picture depicts Ellen and William Craft, wife and husband, circa mid-1800s. Ellen, a "light skinned slave," posed as a male slave owner, and William posed as her slave, in a daring plot to escape from the South to gain their freedom." (See Photo Credits)

Here is the essential problem with including non-Afrikans within the Afrikan group due to some ill-advised allegiance or sense of "fair-play". The woman in the picture is obviously white. There is no question about it. So, many questions arise from this. For instance, why did this enslaved man see it as acceptable to marry this white woman in the midst of all of the suffering that Afrikan women were undergoing all around him at the time? How could a white woman have gotten away with calling herself a "light-skinned slave" if not for the ill-conceived definition of Afrikans that whites created and the acceptance of such by Afrikans themselves? They lived in England after they eloped, so my question is, why not go to Africa? If indeed they both are Black, logic would say that they both should fit right in there. You might say, "Oh well, at least they escaped slavery and they got the story out to other people about the horrors of Afrikan enslavement." But, I would respond that the stories of the horrors of slavery were already well known at the time. Not least of which because of the white author Harriet Beecher's Stowe's book "Uncle Tom's Cabin" which was published in the same period (1852). What this looks like to me is two people capitalizing off of the suffering and misery of Afrikan people for personal gain. Get ready for a movie to be made of this story because this fits the narrative perfectly of what whites and negros are trying to create. Namely, that of star-crossed love between whites and Blacks that can succeed against all odds of hate and division at that time and now. This fits the narrative rapaciously promoted now that the best mate for an Afrikan man or woman is a white person, or at the very least a "light-skinned Black" person. According to *Wikipedia*, after the civil war, these people returned to the USA and tried to live off of handouts from the new political class in power during the era known as Reconstruction, but it came to naught after the election of 1876 and the institution of "Jim Crow" laws. Incidentally, at least three of their five children are likely to have married white people. Two stayed in England, and of the three who moved back to the USA with them, one married a white man who was appointed Collector of the Port of Charleston by Theodore Roosevelt.

33

"I got Indian in my family"

Some people claim that they are not Afrikan because they have some mysterious (American) Indian ancestor who infiltrated their bloodline and turned them into a street-talking, neck-rolling, high yellow, "Black" person with "good hair". I am sorry to say but this is preposterous. Whether or not one or a few American Indians bred with one's Afrikan antecedents is not so much the issue. The real issue is an inability to disavow one or two people of one's genetic background for what one claims is the majority of one's genetic makeup which gives one the ability to confer the racial classification of "Black" onto oneself. In other words, what makes a supposedly Black person elevate one wayward Indian to the level of such power that, through one instance of interbreeding several generations ago, one must now claim that they are "part Indian." Is this truly sane behavior? Is it a rational and scientific explanation of one's genetic heritage? Or, is it what I suspect it to be, an avoidance of responsibility for being an Afrikan. I am really referring here to people who claim an historic ancestry, not a direct parent or grandparent who is still alive today or recently deceased. So, regardless of whether or not one indeed does have admixture in one's genetic contributors of the past, the point of this passage is to shed light a phenomenon which has not been understood by Afrikan people for quite some time. That is the existence of the *intergenerational mulatto*.

The intergenerational mulatto or multiracial person is a person who has authentic, noticeable (to a greater or lesser degree) Afrikan ancestry, but does not display all or even most of the traits of Afrikan people. However, due to the legal history of the expatriate colonial states such as the USA, these people are wrongly categorized as Black. In order to complete this impersonation, many of them adopt a speaking cadence and vernacular associated with inner-city urban dwellers commonly referred to as "talking Black". Irrespective of the fact that not all Afrikan people speak in that way, for some reason in the USA, if one is multi-racial and talks in this way, people readily identify the person as Black. The main problem with this person, *the intergenerational mulatto*, is that it provides the skin-tone cover for whites and other people without Afrikan ancestry to infiltrate our communities and organizations under the guise that they are also Black or "identify as Black", respect Black culture, want to help Black people, or a number of other reasons we have for not identifying them for who they REALLY are…a non-Afrikan person with deep and potentially damaging psychological issues.

Afrikan people commonly display such low-self-esteem and low expectations that we view it as flattering when a non-Afrikan person decides to go "slumming" with us, as it were. Instead of being cautiously kind to the person and being careful not to include them in any of our fundamental relations and official functions, we often welcome them in and then either expect them to take the lead or wait for them to do so, because we do not want to make them think that we are rejecting them on the basis of racial classification. After all, we Afrikans were rejected for centuries which allowed other groups to build up empires and thriving economies, so the last thing we would want to do now is reject others for the same criterion. I mean, it might make them feel bad.

People who state that they have some other heritage other than Afrikan and either possess or do not possess the traits of an Afrikan need to be rejected on either genetic reasons or psychological reasons. If a person is obviously not an Afrikan then fine, they can claim whatever smorgasbord of ancestors they want, but if the person is Afrikan, proper psychological and social health would dictate that the person treats their Afrikan heritage with the highest regard and not even refer to any other ancestry, if any truly exists. This helps the Afrikan group focus on the particular people we want to empower. It helps the group focus on the particular people with whom they want to interrelate. It limits the disorientation of meeting someone whom you think is on board with the Afrikan Sovereignty Project[10] only to find out that they have to attend a sweat lodge or pow-wow first in order to ask their Indian ancestors for permission before they help Afrikan people gain power[11].

Moreover, I have yet to see one person who claims Indian ancestry in their family's past produce a living full-blooded Indian relative to corroborate their claim. I have yet to see one of these people talk intelligently and capably about the specific Indian nation from which their ancestors came or even speak the Indian language competently. I also ask the questions, where are your casinos and why don't you bring your Afrikan family into business with you? What value is it claiming Indian ancestry when whites can claim this ancestry also and reap financial and political rewards from a functionally destroyed people? ACBN seeks to avoid the same fate for Afrikans.

The fact is that most of these intergenerational mulattoes with "Indian in their family" are simply people whose Afrikan ancestors chose the lightest-skinned, mixed-race person or mulatto that they could find to mate with. This *light-skin fetish* continues unabated down through the ages to today, which has resulted in producing someone who looks like Steph Curry or Chris Brown; both men being multi-racial individuals who incorrectly "identify" as Black.

Why this is important?

The importance of pointing out this distinction is numerous and multi-faceted which should be covered in a book of its own. Nevertheless, I will highlight a few benefits of limiting the focus of constituents in the Afrikan Sovereignty Project to actual biological Afrikans. First, and probably most importantly, is that it has a psychological benefit for Afrikan people. Afrikan people have been dismissed, marginalized, and ridiculed for possessing Afrikan traits[12]. Several derogatory names have been hurled at Afrikan people for these traits by first whites, and then by Afrikans and multi-racial people imitating the behavior of whites. Afrikan men misdirect their rage and energy into trying to impress white men and other mentacidal[13] Afrikan men that they can attain the sexual favors of an imitation white woman or and actual European female instead of focusing on building healthier relationships with Black women as their ideal mate and organizing with other Black men to build a system of social relations through industrial, technological, institutional, financial, and security organizations. Afrikan women have responded to this asinine tendency of Afrikan men by adopting beauty standards to gain the attention of Afrikan men which make them look quite ridiculous and obvious in their attempt to imitate the biological features of non-Afrikan women. The most apparent method of doing this is by either wearing fake hair, or chemically damaging their natural hair in an effort to compete with European and Asian women for the affection of Afrikan men. There are other reasons for this as well, such as an effort to raise their general level of self-esteem as women in a racist society, but Afrikan women on the continent are not immune from this behavior either. So, it indicates a widespread psychological malady *vis-à-vis* the Afrikan self-perception and the comparison we have with ourselves to other powerful racial groups on the planet. We seek to be accepted by them without having the power to demand their respect. Instead of displaying our natural features and directing our energy towards building healthy relationships and thereby establishing a power base for Afrikan people, we avoid this noble aim for the fleeting immediacy of momentary glee.

Another benefit would be to raise the value of having Afrikan features themselves. By accepting any person as Black, (even whites and Asians based upon the faddish scientific view that '*we are all Afrikan*" posited by people promoting a decidedly political interpretation of the Theory of Evolution[14]) we devalue Afrikanity to the point of meaninglessness. If anyone can be a part of the group, then the group has no particular basis for organizing to improve its condition—especially the people possessing authentic Afrikan traits mentioned in the beginning of this chapter. The increase in the value of Afrikan features would likely change the present course of Afrikan men seeking to create offspring which do not resemble them in the hopes that their mixed-race kids will have a better chance of success in life both economically and socially. This can convince Afrikan men to value their looks and replicate themselves with their authentic traits via the Afrikan woman who is the only woman on the planet who has the power to facilitate this. Of course, this would also raise the value of Afrikan women. The increased value in the pair-mating possibilities of Afrikan men and Afrikan women can have several positive implications such as healthier communities, healthier levels of intra-racial activities to build institutions to sustain life, and a clearer socio-political vision of the group whose survival is at stake, and who should be the primary beneficiaries of policy and programs created by Afrikan people to help Afrikan people[15a,15b]. The present course Afrikans are on, woefully focuses on rewarding anti-social behavior, sexual fetishism, and self-hate. It also limits the punishment which can be meted out socially to traitors who sully Afrikanity by giving in to individualistic needs of ego and sexual gratification.

Furthermore, by accepting any person as Afrikan, as I have stated, we hamper our ability to punish those Afrikans whose behavior betrays group interest. We have no ability to ostracize or prevent Afrikan traitors from participation in our affairs. If we, in one breath say that interracial relationships are a negative activity among Afrikans who seek acceptance by foreign groups, and then at the same time say that the mulatto or mixed-race offspring of such unions are Afrikan, we are promoting an inherent contradiction in our stance. This contradiction, if left unresolved, will not allow us to be taken seriously by Afrikan people nor by our enemies and competitors against whom we say we are seeking to balance the levels of power and restore our political standing in the world. We act as though our enemies and competitors are simply congenitally racist, and do not study our present and historical behavior to determine how best to exploit and manipulate us. Our adherence to the hypodescent rule or the *"one-drop rule"*[16] allows foreign exploiters to simply mate with an Afrikan person, produce a mixed-race offspring, train that offspring to value non-Afrikan cultures and societies over Afrikan culture and society, then seed that person back into Afrikan societies when the time is right to act as a sleeper agent to awake at the perfect moment and help facilitate the transfer of wealth and power to the non-Afrikan group from the Afrikan group. At the very least, these mixed-race individuals act as a foil to distract our efforts at organization and mobilization so we will remember that "it is not all white people" who are hateful towards us simply due to the fact that their parent was a European, Indian, Lebanese, Asian, Arab, and so on.

38

A psychologically healthy individual who has a proper relationship with one's parents and surrounding community of racially congruent individuals would value these relationships and experiences and want to see these types of people live on into the distance future. We would not want to see these people diminished and eliminated on the altar of a fantasy of a raceless society to exist at some unknown point in the future. We would live for the day to see our grandparents and great-grandparents reflected in the faces of our children. If we did indeed have these psychologically healthy social experiences on a wider scale, we would not be undergoing the phenomenon of people leaving the neighborhoods and communities where they were raised and subsequently travelling to far off places to marry the person with the least amount of Afrikan features as possible, only to return to the area from which they are from to try and receive praise for their non-Afrikan mating choice. We would not welcome rejects and individuals from the lowest level of social status in foreign groups into our communities and societies who only have the "virtue" of being non-Black. Thus, we attempt to gain favor by signaling to ourselves, and any non-Black who cares to notice, that we have a higher morality than they do. This continues even though we would have to struggle to identify one material benefit these people from the dregs of foreign societies have contributed to the Afrikan project for sovereignty and power. Among healthy individuals, the preservation of one's biogenetic inheritance is of supreme importance.

To illustrate this last point, I will discuss a few anecdotes. Once I was in Japan, and I had a need to buy a few things at the grocery store. When I was in the store I saw a family of three generations shopping for various items. The mother and the grandmother were discussing the things that they should buy and the mother had a newborn infant with her. Presumably, the man who was her father, and also the grandfather of the child, was holding the infant while the women shopped. During this time, I noticed that the grandfather was singing what seemed like an old and traditional Japanese song into the ear of the baby. He was singing at a low volume, almost imperceptibly, but I realized at that time that this is one important way how culture is passed on. The child during this very important neurological development stage will adhere to positive feelings of the culture being transmitted by the grandfather. Hence, the Japanese grandfather's biogenetic future is assured by creating a new generation of Japanese who value the traditions and identity of the culture. He is doing this while his daughter and wife fulfill other functions of maintaining Japanese life, namely securing food for the family. This is the interconnected way that a biogenetic group functions to ensure its survival. Now imagine if the child were mixed-race. Sure, the same act could occur, but what are the implications? Because the child would have only one side of the family as Japanese, they would be missing the cultural legacy of the non-Japanese side. This would always be a void in the psyche of the person as they grew to adulthood. Since, as I stated, the biogenetic and cultural inheritance is neurologically based (that is to say, we access the thoughts, ideas, and emotions of culture in our brain and engage in corresponding activity using our five senses and neuronal sensitivities), the mixed-race person would always be seeking to compensate in one way or another for the lack of one or more of these inheritances, or to attain the one which was lacking in the first place. The pure Japanese child never has to encounter this confusion and is congenitally created to be Japanese. The Japanese child is not created to be Japanese when it suits the Japanese body politic and then be non-Japanese when it is more convenient to do so. It is biologically and genetically part of the culture at the basis of its biological self and world perception. This is its biogenetic inheritance which it then has the duty and responsibility of passing on. Unlike the mixed-race product of confused and/or self-hating Afrikans, this particular Japanese family has taken it upon itself to create more Japanese people. It has not produced ambiguous Japanese and then engaged in accusing other Japanese people who are truly fulfilling their duties, to also accept their mixed-Japanese as Japanese, and if they don't, then charge them with committing a socio-emotional transgression of "hate" or "discrimination". Logically speaking, it would be the Japanese engaged in miscegenation based "mixed-racism"[17] that has committed the offense. To further bolster this point, on another occasion during my time in Japan, I saw a small child about the age of 5 or 6 who was a multi-racial girl of Afrikan and Japanese genetic contributions. I was on the train and minding my own business when her Japanese mother and she entered. The child saw me and was curious and started to inch toward the position on the train where I was standing. I looked at the mother to see if she would retrieve her child from approaching a stranger. She did not. She apparently wanted her daughter to have some sort of interaction with an Afrikan man so that she would know something of how to relate to Afrikans when the time came in her life later to do so. This was her attempt to foist upon me, a stranger, the responsibility of socializing her half-Japanese/half-Afrikan daughter for her. However, I had no involvement in the degeneracy associated with her decision to destroy her genetics and mate with an Afrikan man who had an Asian woman fetish. This shows that the implications of this behavior are known by people who practice this racial amalgamation, but they want others to support their decisions after the fact and solidify their half-witted hope for a raceless society in the future. I ignored the multi-racial girl and exited the train at the next stop.

Another revelation of this incident is the realization that people do not make choices about with whom to procreate in a social vacuum. There choices impact others in the society on many levels, particularly psychologically and genetically. However, people in these IRs avoid these ramifications and count on others being cowed into accepting their peculiarities.

To conclude this portion on the importance of recognizing authentic Afrikans as such, I would like to relay another anecdote. I had the occasion to encounter another mixed-race Japanese and Afrikan woman about the age of 18 or 19. She could only speak Japanese because assumedly her father had since vacated Japan before she could learn whichever language he spoke. She was obviously not Afrikan because of her hair, which was decidedly the Asian type. She wore the fashionable clothes that young Japanese women typically wore, but was quite reserved in her personality. She was a loner, and if she had friends, she rarely interacted with them. This was based on the fact that I had no occasion to see her with any friends or a clique of people with whom she socialized—although I often saw other people her age commonly socializing with their friends and acquaintances. Her skin was just outside the color spectrum for Afrikan people and she would be mistaken for an Afrikan with 'good hair' in places like the US, the UK, or the Caribbean. However, I noticed her social awkwardness and it was similar to the general social awkwardness that Japanese exhibit. However, I surmised that this particular awkwardness had a racial component to it. It is not that other Japanese were outright and overtly rude to her, but both she and they knew that she was not Japanese. She had not ability to pass on the biogenetic inheritance of Japanese people within her. So, if she marries a Japanese man, it is likely that they will live abroad from Japan. But, I suspect that she will eventually drift either towards marrying or procreating with an Afrikan man who has a multiracial sexual fetish, and then living in a place like Canada, or do the same with a lascivious white male with a sexual fetish for swarthy women whom he would like to house to be at his beck and call when it fancies him. Either way it goes for her, and the young child I mentioned before, their biogenetic inheritance is highly questionable, and in the fullness of time they must adopt a socio-political view that justifies their existence. It is the same for all people, which is why I am advocating for such a clear and focused view for Afrikans at this time in history. Not to do so would likely end in utter destruction for Afrikan people as we have been known since time immemorial. It has been quipped that "tradition is the illusion of permanence"[18]. But indeed, there are some constants that do not change with time. Outer appearances or generally accepted behavior might change, but certain traits that have been infused into a biogenetic group within the cauldron of time do not change without first a change in perception and then behavior. We Afrikans have the power to control these biological constants, so I am writing this book to give reason and rationality to seizing this control for the present age and for ages to come. Specifically, a control over our procreative power which has been viciously wrestled from us through colonization and slavery.

Chapter 2: The Destructive Nature of Interracial Relationships

Overall tackiness and perversion of interracial relationships

I would like to delve briefly into the matter of interracial relationships (IR). For a fuller exploration of this matter, I would recommend the book "The Interracial Con-Game" written by Trojan Pam. She beautifully and insightfully explores this issue in detail, so I will just give a few passing remarks and observations about the subject here. In my view all IRs, whether they be marriage, dating, or simply sexual, are the product of deep and unresolved psychological issues in both parties involved. Due to the inherent differences in biology, genetics, culture, history, and the particular group psychology of one's ethnic origin, we have to fundamentally question the basis for the relationships of people interracially involved. I would posit the notion that these relationships are based primarily on money or a sexual fetish. They are not based on the other factors which must be present to make a healthy relationship work which is why they typically end in divorce[1]. I often see people who are in these relationships make overt attempts to be recognized by people in their immediate vicinity which to me indicates that the component of societal approval is lacking in most of these relationships. Two people do not just "get married". Two families actually are doing the bonding and families reside in the larger community. So, if people in these relationships are not getting the required approval that all normal and healthy relationships require and normally receive as a matter of course, then this need is expressed through antagonism towards individuals of one or the other's racial group who do not happen to look on approvingly and enviously. People in IRs go through outrageous efforts to be noticed, and if they do not receive the attention, they then charge unfounded claims of bias, and hostility on the part of the person or people ignoring them. This is an indication of the psychological phenomenon known as *projection*. Their projection is usually due to a feeling of inferiority for having put their sexual fetish on display for the world, or by indicating to the general public that they will stoop to any low level of behavior in order to receive material goods or psychological approval from a member of another race who is in a different social position.

Another form of tackiness often displayed by people in IRs is to assume that they are engaged in a cutting edge, and enlightened form of social relations. They often claim that they are engaged in creating a "new race" which will be light brown and result in the end of racism. It strikes me as odd that these confused people think that the solution to power differentials between racial groups is by committing the act of coitus. People apparently think it is possible to *fuck* their problems away. This must be seen for what it is. A distinct and acute form of lunacy. Sexual relations are inherently based on power differentials anyway, so how is it possible that the lack of collective power that Afrikans have is going to be corrected by a white or Asian man or woman creating a hybrid child with an Afrikan? This has never been fully explained by people who religiously engage in and cling to the idea of IRs being the salvation of man.

There are also people in IRs who are astonishingly apolitical. They think that their actions have no consequences and that others should just accept their behavior and sickness. Some people will even violently defend their right to destroy social cohesion and genetic stability. Their ravenous anger and hate is truly on display when they are in defense of their sexual activities. It is rather ironic that these people claim that their choice in mate should not matter to others, but then demand that others cater to their choices. These people disregard any social or political implications of their selections on the basis of their right to "individual choice", and that "individuals" can choose what they want and it has no further impact. However, they do want their hybrid kids to be accepted and taught. They want to be gainfully employed and housed. This all requires a relationship with the larger community. So, if no one's opinion and desires matter other than that of the individual's, don't then other "individuals" have the right to deny you the accommodations you seek? It is a highly hypocritical position, and in order to facilitate such a viewpoint, it necessitates large government intervention and protection through legislation,

44

media promotion, and ideological coercion. All of this is unnoticed by these "individuals" who claim they are making their own decisions.

Why Black men date non-Black women

The standard reasons that Afrikan men give to justify the need to date non-Afrikan women are quite bereft of foundational logic, but are continually repeated ad nauseam so that they can maintain their unresolved urge to engage in unbridled sexual fetishism. Such reasons are the following ridiculous notions expressed by the Afrikan man saying something like, "*I can't help who I fall in love with*" or "*I don't see color*". Black men also justify this weakness for pale vaginas by saying that "*We are all people*" or "*We are all god's children*". The inanest of all of these kinds of self-serving justifications which is typically uttered by the most mis-educated and intellectually dishonest among us is when he says "*race is just a social construct*". Therefore, we are to think that this Afrikan man is supposedly not taking *race* into account when making a mate selection because "*that would be racist*". When asked about what else the individual is doing to combat "racism" the person asking the question is usually met with blank stares, or even worse given a circumlocutive, rambling barrage of nonsense to explain away why the IR fetishist's perverted sexual desire is not actually an untreated psychological illness, but that one is really engaged in the process of "*transcending race*" by "*loving all people*" and starting with the white woman in his bed at present. I would encourage readers to obtain a copy of the book "Black Skins, White Masks"[2] written by psychiatrist Franz Fanon; a Black man who regrettably married a white woman himself. Be that as it may, he delves into the subject quite skillfully and even though his focus is on Afrikan men during the colonial period in the Caribbean, some of his insights can be generalized to Afrikan men globally. I will mention a few pertinent issues regarding this subject here.

The first and most important reason is the psychological issue of self-hate. We often hear this offered as a reason why Black men date interracially, but we must not treat it as a cliché. Very often Afrikan men feel scorn cast towards them either directly or indirectly because of their Afrikan looks and the miniscule amount of political-economic influence they have both socially and at the institutional level. Images circulated in the media have not moved far from the basic description of Afrikans as unrefined, criminals with malintent for whites and their "civilization". With this constant barrage of imagery, projected globally now, it trains others (including other Black people) to fear the Afrikan man as a threat. This is the basic reason that white and Asian women clutch their handbags when Afrikan men walk by and why Afrikan men and women are followed in the stores and receive curt and inferior service while shopping at various locations. These images are reinforced in the socialization that Afrikan men often experience by peers during key stages of life. If the Afrikan man is raised around non-Afrikan people, they often treat him as a mascot of sorts, and ask him questions about Blackness that they feel he is qualified to answer because he is Black. He is often made to laugh at jokes told by his white peers at the expense of Blacks in order to display his fealty to the whites and made to acknowledge certain stereotypes and preconceived notions the whites have about Black people. This set of experiences builds up to point where he may wish that he was not Black, or that Black people did not have such traits which whites and others can use to malign him personally, or wish that he did not have to participate in these awkward social interactions.

If the Afrikan man grew up around other Black people, and they are not from a very affluent neighborhood, embarrassment for being Black and poor together with being addicted to the consumption of images of successful and prosperous whites shown on television might create a distorted view of reality and instill the misguided goal of attaining friendship and favor with whites in order to partake in the perceived benefits of white society, as opposed to developing his own affluent society of Afrikan people. Very often, young Afrikan men assume that there are no affluent Afrikan areas in which to seek more comfort and stability, so a white environment is pursued to the exclusion of all others.

There is also the issue of pornography which displays rampant images of the most vulgar and lewdest sexual peccadilloes that have been created by the white mind. If a young Afrikan male is exposed to this at an early age and develops a psychological dependency on watching these movies, this can turn into an urge to experience some of the acts that are depicted in these videos. In many of these video series, the sex acts displayed focus on a Afrikan man with a large penis ravaging some non-Afrikan female. If we connect the ingestion of all of these negative images and social experiences to surmise a psychological profile that white media and society are trying to create in the minds of Afrikan men, we can conclude that it wants to disempower the ability of Afrikan men to be intellectually self-creative, and biogenetically regenerative, by forestalling us from creating power systems in relations with other Afrikan men, and instead promoting the idea of ourselves as the individual Black stud, capable of miraculous feats of sportsmanship and sexual conquest. Hence, men who hate the mainstream image of the unenterprising, antisocial Black male from poverty, can aspire to become a sexual dynamo, and faux representation of bravado for salacious white and other non-Afrikan women to use as a sexual plaything. This relieves some of the psychological malady of the Afrikan man, but it never actually solves the problem. In this scenario created by white people, the best outcome an Afrikan man can attain is a series of sexual trysts with non-Afrikan women, or even producing a mixed-race kid, but the reversal of the powerlessness he actual seeks to establish is never realized. He then ultimately finds himself living in a culture of society which is still run and maintained by other groups of men; few to none of which are from his racial group. He may find himself living in a society or environment where he is the only negro or one of a handful. These other non-Afrikan people often mildly tolerate him, but never actually allow him to be anything more than the mascot or "special negro" which that society retrieved from the backwards culture that birthed him. They feel that he may have the wherewithal to live in the foreign society with his foreign bride, but they make sure that he knows he is never *of the society*. His foreign bride and mixed-race kid(s) are his consolation prizes for the foreign society having saved

47

and protected him from his savage kin. He rewards them with an infusion of ancient genetics to increase their group's future fertility and to use a hybrid to confuse and entice other Afrikan men with skills desired the foreign group (brain drain) to leave their racial group and help build and maintain a foreign one.

Afrikan men also want to impress others, especially white men, on the type of sexual mate they were able to attain. They do this to doubly reinforce the white created stereotype of the Black male sexual dynamo, and to effeminately and passively "get back" at whites for having destroyed their nations and distinction as a group of men. By showing off the rejected obese or scrawny woman of white society as their sex mates (or even if a white woman they have might be somewhat attractive) they can let other white men know that they have sexual access to all of the various non-Afrikan women, *and particularly the white woman,* which white men have had access to since the beginning of global colonialization. Afrikan men are deluded by thinking that this ability to have sex with non-Afrikan women puts them on an equal plane as whites, Asians, and other organized groups of men who have created power systems which influence the daily lives of people around the world. But in actually fact, the display of these sexual interludes does nothing to change the basic view of Black men most others have. In fact, it confirms a view already held by others of the lack of sexual discipline Afrikan men have. So, in an ultimate irony, by clinging to the image of the *strapping sexual dynamo*, they verify the ideas of inferiority held by others and do not actually change their situation or garner the social respect they seek.

Many Afrikan men place a higher value on women with pale skin than they do on women with a normal Afrikan skin tone. The media serves in this purpose as well, by promoting pale and slightly swarthy women who are racially ambiguous and referring to them as Black, African-American, or in some cases as Afrikan even though the person might be mixed, or not have any Afrikan ancestry at all. The former pop singer Paula Abdul comes to mind in this regard. She has no Afrikan ancestry whatsoever, but was thought of as a "Black" female when she was first presented on the music scene. A more recent case is the actress Jessica Alba whom many thought was "Black" as well. If some women display traits traditionally associated with Afrikan people such as musical ability, large lips, or a rotund figure, they are referred to as "Black" or it is claimed that they have some hidden Afrikan ancestry. Mariah Carey is one such woman who has a very unique singing ability, but has a white mother and a multiracial father, however she is referred to as "Black" and was put before the Black music buying audience as a "Black artist". Another woman, whom shall remain nameless, is also photographed with several Afrikan boyfriends. Given her constant exposure on her reality show which she does with other oddball members of her family, some people actually claim that she has Afrikan ancestry because of the size and shape of her lower body. This constant stream of images implying that these white and racially ambiguous women are the ideal mate for Afrikan men creates a mental connection in easily influenced Afrikan men between sexual satisfaction, happiness, and the non-Afrikan woman. The sexual act is primarily a neurological function, so based on how the mind is organized and what values and tastes have been created through various socialization processes, but by no less degree through media influence, it can be concluded that by promoting the non-Afrikan woman as the premier standard of sexually-charged beauty for Black men, men consciously and subconsciously seek to satisfy this desire by attaining what they wrongly view is a more pleasurable type of woman, even though it is not. They base their choice of mate on an externally created, flawed and foreign set of criteria which is separate from both the reality and the implications of one's sexual choices. The purpose of sex is procreation, but is has a pleasurable component as well. Given this dual nature, much care and planning must go into one's sexual partner with an interest on the future development of the child and the social relations which will be affected by this. Since this is the case, making a sexual mate selection solely based on images created by foreign groups of people (principally whites and others who call themselves Jews), and standards of behavior modelled by people with very questionable morals and intelligence, (i.e. actors, comedians, and sports stars) is very circumspect to say the least.

Why Black women date non-Black men

Again, I will just touch on only a few issues here. I would recommend that readers acquire the book *"The Beauty Con-Game"*[3] also written by Trojan Pam and the book *"Excuses, Excuses: The Politics of Interracial Coupling"*[4] written by Mwalimu K. Bomani Baruti to get a more explicit understanding of this phenomenon. Both books are well-written and quite easy to read in a few days or so, but they focus more directly on the subject of this chapter. Remember, this book is about **ACBN**: *Afrikan-Centered Biological Nationalism*, but I discuss these issues because I think the topics in this chapter are related to **ACBN,** so I think it is proper to make some statements about them before returning to the subject of this present book.

With that said, I will unequivocally state that Afrikan women's reasons are too lacking logic given the historical circumstances involving Afrikan women and Eurasian men. It is due to historical amnesia and a lack of the transference of historical knowledge through Afrikan-centered institutions that creates the basis for Afrikan women even considering being with white and other non-Black men. The history of Black women's interaction with them is replete with bondage, rape, kidnapping, torture, exploitation, and lack of any expression of general adoration or respect for the natural beauty of Black women. Dr. Amos Wilson has written extensively about how amnesia creates the psychological conditions necessary to fall victim to suggestions of all types and to engage in acts, which with the full knowledge of one's own past, one would avoid due to the clear and demonstrated historical outcomes.[5]

Many Afrikan women also use the mantra of *"not being able to see color"*. It would behoove these women to see an ophthalmologist rather that sleeping with and marrying white men. However, let us say that they are using this statement as a metaphor. Don't you find it odd that the other typical excuse used by Afrikan women is that they can't find any Black men "on their level" in order to substantiate their decision to engage in intimate relations with white, Arab, and other non-Black men? Apparently, *they do* see color in this regard, but their ability to see the color of the mate they ultimately chose to be with was impaired in some way. It indicates that there are some psychological contortions occurring here. Let me explain further.

I would like to deal with the second most popular reason given by these women first. The lack of suitable Black men. Some women may want to believe this to be the case in some circumstances, but I would add a statement for your consideration made by a Black woman regarding the competition they are receiving from non-Afrikan women for attention of Afrikan men. This particular woman mentioned that non-Afrikan women are less demanding and critical on the Afrikan man concerning his general daily behavior[6]. This doesn't mean that *anything goes*, but it means that if basic contributions by the man are met in the relationship, (e.g. financial, sexual, companionship, social), then the non-Afrikan woman overlooks other personality traits or issues which might be bothersome, but are not so irritating as to serve as a basis for neurotic and unrelenting criticism, attempts to change the man, or to end the relationship. In short, I am saying that some of the expectations Afrikan women have are unreasonably high for Afrikan men and they use the inability for the man to reach these heights as a justification for endless ridicule and condescension. This helps to make the man susceptible to the easy comfort of a non-Black female who will fulfill most of his needs, but with little of the accompanying stress of not being "on their mate's level". Of course, I am not excusing the Afrikan man for bad and unacceptable behavior, nor blaming the Afrikan woman for having some standards, but what often is the case is that these Afrikan women who date white men or other non-Black men have far lower standards of behavior for these non-Black men to meet. In fact, most of these women take a very submissive position regarding non-Black men and are very combative with Black men whom they date and/or interact with in general. The fact is that these women are guided by the strong and powerful fantasy of being treated as if they are non-Black themselves by the non-Black mate. They want to experience the favor bestowed on white women which is depicted in the fantasy of movies, TV shows, and popular songs. They want to be surrounded by the material comfort they associate with the white world, and so they do mental acrobatics to obviate the reality that **whites build communities and institutions for white people primarily**. Hence, these Black women are typically very religiously Christian, Muslim (Sunni or Shi'a, *not Nation of Islam...yet*), or socially and politically liberal, and devote a lot of lip service to social justice causes and charities. Most of these causes have little to do with actually helping Black people directly, but the mention of them can gain them regard for their sense of morality within the white community of her husband or boyfriend. They engage in this discourse relentlessly in the hopes that they will receive reciprocal moral regard by whites, which usually does not happen. What often happens is the Black women faces back-handed compliments and social slights for being Black. She ignores these as much as possible in order to maintain her relationship with the white man. Sometimes she is even ridiculed or serves as the butt of racist jokes by the man's friends or family and she must accept these attempts at humor without being offended or else she is the one who will be charged with racial hatred and antagonism. Because after all, "*they were only joking!*" The husband or mate typically defends their friends over the feelings of the Black woman because at the end of the day, the man sees the woman as a sexual conquest who is given the privilege of actually sharing the abode of his superior culture. The logic follows that if she did not agree that he and his culture **are** superior, then she would not be with a white man in the first place, right?

Therefore, the point the woman was making, whose statement I paraphrased earlier, and that I am reiterating and expounding upon now, is that Afrikan women, likely due to psychological issues of self-perception, low self-esteem, and after focusing relentlessly on attaining the colonial education and social acceptance offered by Euro-centered, owned and operated, educational institutions, then thinks of herself as having reached a status above and beyond that of her natural counterpart, and seeks to have this reflected in her choice of mate—the white man. The main problem with this is that her mate

52

never truly acknowledges her experience and distinctive history as a Black woman. Even if the non-Afrikan man the woman is with is able to recall facts and dates about it, in the end, it is the woman whose untreated psychosis regarding her Black identity is left to fester and she must adopt the anti-Black rationale of the white man's (or other man's) culture. The irony here is that she would have had to adopt the rationale and worldview of the Black man anyway, which (when both are healthy) would have been much more complimentary to her <u>actual</u> psycho-history[7], but she refuses to do so based on self-abnegation and a rejection of the Black male as having any ability to be someone she could respect.

Another reason Afrikan women date white and other non-Black men is due to their misplaced nurturing instinct. These women hate or at least have a disdain for the natural beauty of Afrikan people (and sometimes themselves), so they want to erase it by having mixed children. They think mixed children are more beautiful than Afrikan children. Personally, (if I may editorialize for a moment) the vast majority of mixed-race people (individuals with one Afrikan and one white or non-Afrikan parent) look like genetic mutants to me. The few that could be viewed as attractive are promoted in the media to present the illusion that all products of race-mixing are potential models, actresses, or actors. People see these images and then propagate the lie through daily conversations wherein they express their "personal opinions" about the supposed intrinsic aesthetic superiority of mixed-race people. Consider the following quote for example:

"I love white guys. I actually **don't** date Black guys. I just *have a thing* for white boys. A little vanilla and a little chocolate, *they make cute babies.*" ~Ariane Andrew (Black) former WWE entertainer.

After being challenged for the vile nature of her statement, she later said the following:

"I never said ***I don't*** [date Black men] …My intentions were just pretty much saying that I have a preference. At the end of the day…when you look at somebody, it's in the eye of the beholder. So, to me, at the end of the day, it's about personality. If I vibe with you, I vibe with you."[8]

There so much psychobabble going on in that statement, it is almost too much to analyze. It also might take another book just to dissect her contradictions and assumptions. But, we can rest assured that this woman **does in fact see color**. According to her, apparently relationships are mostly about 'personality and vibes'. So, to all of you Black men out there trying to figure out what Black women want, take her advice and work on developing your personality and 'vibing skills'. I hope the above quote indicates how dangerous it is to listen to advice and viewpoints from <u>individuals who get paid to help other people forget about the reality of their lives by providing entertainment to them</u>. However, the female sports entertainer went on to say that she has dated a Black man in the past but, "he...*it* got verbally abusive." Although she does not attribute this verbal abuse to race, nevertheless, the result is a prohibition on dating Afrikan men due to *one* experience with *one* Black man that she mentioned. I find it interesting that even though numerous white celebrities have been involved with multiple romantic partners in what I refer to as serial monogamous relationships—that is dating or marrying one person after another in a string of intimate pairings—I, *personally*, have never heard one of these white people say that they will never date a white person again. Of course, I have heard white people voice their sexual fetish for Afrikan, Mestizo, or Asian people, but as far as a high-profile celebrity stating, after being married or involved multiple times with other white people, that they **don't** or **will never again** date another white person, that particular novelty has eluded my ears. It is only Afrikan people whom I have heard say this, and it is usually after *one bad experience*. Elizabeth Taylor, Brad Pitt, Warren Beatty, Mia Farrow, Zsa Zsa Gabor, Mickey Rooney, Larry King, Lana Turner, Tony Curtis, Doris Day, Christie Brinkley, Liza Minelli, Tom Cruise, Drew Barrymore, Kate Winslet, Frank Sinatra, Brittany Spears, Demi Moore, Joan Collins, Sean Penn, Mick Jagger, James Cameron, Judy Garland, and many more unmentioned here have all notoriously been married to or dated many other white people. After all the marriages, relationships, children, and even the media circuses that have been generated around some of their break-ups ended, I have not heard one of the aforementioned people state publicly that they are done with marrying white people, or they don't date white people anymore. By the way, please don't try to point to people like Robert DeNiro and Bill Maher. It is obvious that they have sexual fetishes and many of the women they dated or married were mixed-race, so it is obvious that they look for women who specifically do not have the social or financial power to challenge their authority in a sexual relationship. Their interest is more about perversion and power that anything else, not "love". And it is much less about helping Afrikan people. Also, please don't mention Madonna, she *ONLY* married white men, and slept with non-white men in an attempt to get them to father some mixed-race children that she coveted. Do you really think that this absurd desire of Madonna's was healthy and mentally well-balanced? Are her half-breed children (by a non-white mestizo) and the adopted Afrikan children going to be of any value to the Afrikan project for sovereign power? Or will they just serve to confuse non-white people even more and adhere to the "angelic nature" of white celebrities who graciously laid down with a non-white person to give the world a hybrid kid? If it is still possible for Madonna to enter and legally kidnap children from Afrikan nations to serve as her *lifestyle accessories*, I highly doubt that these children will be able to realistically help Afrikan people, but this is yet to conclusively be seen. However, I'm not holding my breath. We can only hope that they will someday remember who they are, but at this point, Afrikan people need much more than just hope and white genetics.

Lastly, Afrikan women who marry white men are decidedly *white-identified*. These are the woman who most often claim "*love knows no color*" or that they "*cannot see color*", but it is clear that they can. Let me explain. *White-identification* means that these women aspire to have the internal and external elements associated with white/European cultural sensibilities adorn and expressed in every aspect of their lives and lifestyle. They want to speak multiple European languages, largely for social purposes. That is so they can interact with white people more closely. It is rare that languages are learned so they can speak to more Afrikan people who speak French, Spanish, Portuguese, and so on. They want to wear the high fashion of Europe and frown upon fashion designed and produced in Afrika unless they are wearing it to make a vapid and shallow political statement…usually after following a white person's approved lead. They wear their hair in European or Asian styles and make an overt effort to imitate the speech patterns of Europeans. This does not merely mean speaking the language correctly, they adopt all of the idiosyncratic speech tones, fillers, colloquialisms and phraseologies of European speakers after having specifically studied them on how to do it. Again, this does not mean just speaking the language grammatically correct or having no noticeable "Black" accent, it is an effort to be identical to whites who speak the language if one were not physically seen. These women adopt the strict cultural habits of Europeans. They are not distorted habits with an Afrikan tinge to them such as singing Gospel music by Afrikan people. Christianity is a European religion and Afrikan people adopted it and put their own creativity and imprint onto it. That is not what I am talking about. White-identified women strive to do things exactly as the Europeans do because they think it is the refined and appropriate way to do it, thus making them "better" than other Black people, and thus increases their opportunity to be embraced by *any* random white person as part of the white collective. I am much more talking about the *reasoning* behind what the white-identified woman does, not so much the imitative behavior colonized and enslaved people must adopt to survive which is always distinctive in its character due to cross-cultural and cross-linguistic influences. I am talking about a specific and focused effort to pattern one's behavior, outlook, and lifestyle so it is *indistinguishable* from an average white person except for the fact that one has Afrikan physical features. Then, after this inculcation is complete, in an ultimate attempt to extinguish these corporeal remnants of one's Afrikan past and ancestry, the woman mates with a white man…or a non-Afrikan man as the case may be. *This is the white-identified Afrikan woman.* A woman that avoids seeing or refuses to see the destructive nature that European culture has and continues to have on Afrikan people, she negates the value of

56

anything Afrikan, **and then** marries and procreates with a white man as the *coup de grâce* in wiping out any remaining vestiges of Afrikanity within herself and her immediate surroundings. **This is done to actualize the fact in her mind that white men are better than Afrikan men and that creating the mixed-race kid is the most desirable use of her womb over which Black men have no control—and purposefully so**. The white-identified woman does not challenge the white man's social rank, status, standing, accomplishments, or inherent prestige and power. She accepts it uncritically because by being with him and having his kid, she has attained *whiteness*, which was her ultimate, if unspoken, goal.

For people who will read this a think, "Well all Black people do this on one level or another" or "I've seen Black people who do this and don't marry white people". I am not talking about those people. I am not just talking about the conditions of being politically subjugated by white people under the system of white hegemony[9]. I am talking about people who willfully and due to having made a *specific decision* to do so, eschew Afrikan people from social interactions so that they can *specifically* be more favorable and closer to white people. I am not just talking about Afrikan people with white friends or coworkers. I am not talking about Afrikan people who occasionally watch movies with white actors in them, read books written by whites, or listen to white musical artists. I am talking about Afrikan people who have *consciously decided* that the "solution" to their Blackness or Afrikanity is to be with white people exclusively and for the purposes of marriage and procreation. Therefore, *they have made the decision* to totally acquiesce to white socio-cultural activities as the *sine qua non* of their existence, and view the attainment of a white mate as the ultimate victory in this pursuit. This person, in no uncertain terms, has the ability to see color and acts on it.

Why whites and others date Afrikans

Too many Afrikan people are under the delusion that white people who date Afrikan people are not racist. They think that these people like Black people and are "alright", "safe", "cool", "down" or are one of the elusive "good white people" that are proclaimed by some Blacks to actually exist. Afrikan people who are in these relationships are additionally under the psychosis that they are such a unique individual and unlike other Afrikan people that they qualify to be chosen by this "saintly" white person for a relationship. Rarely, if ever, do Afrikan people actual examine why some whites choose to mate with Afrikan people considering the history of the relationship they have had with Afrikans as a group. They seem to believe that because whites choose to have sex with a Black person that they have undergone some type of enlightened self-discovery, and epiphany of sorts, which separates them from the brutal nature and history of Europe. Afrikans who advocate or enter into these relations also claim that "white people have changed". Afrikans believe that this particular white person is unlike their predecessors and other "racist" white people, and are fit to bring into Afrikan communities, families, and genetic lineages. Nothing could be further from the truth.

Whites and other non-Blacks who date Afrikan people are just as racist and anti-Black as anyone who does not engage in such behavior. The difference is that they have just chosen another way to go about expressing this inherent trait in European (Eurasian) behavior[10]. They detest Afrikan people and Afrikan physical features so much that they want to directly assist in breeding these traits out. I often hear white mothers and fathers of mulatto children state that their child is "Black". A more vicious and racist proclamation could not be made. Who does this person think they are to define Black people for us? To add more insult, they doubly and slyly reject their kid as a member of their own white race. This is a clear indication of how these people think. They think they have the power to remake Afrikans into the image that they desire to see, and not the image which was created by our ancestors through evolutionary strides and experiences on the Afrikan continent from time immemorial.

Regardless of the trope that people repeat claiming that "they can't help whom they fall in love with." These whites and other non-Blacks deliberately choose Afrikans who are gullible, naïve, apathetic, addicted to damaging substances and/or behaviors, and typical have a liberal "live and let live" outlook on humanity. Whites who engage in sexual relations with Afrikan people practice the *racism of low expectations* commonly practiced by socially and sexually liberal whites. They believe that Afrikan people cannot do anything separate and apart from their meddling, so they interject themselves into fundamental Afrikan social relations to disrupt and command the direction, manners of interactions, and thoughts about whites and the world that they want Black people to enshrine. By infusing themselves within the familial relations of Afrikans they can more directly defuse any thoughts which might be aimed at self-actualization among Afrikans in general. In other words, they limit the ability for the least confused and most committed members of the Afrikan family to advocate for correct thinking and behavior without having to be distracted by a direct challenge from either the white person or the Afrikan in the lascivious relationship with the white/non-Black person. Moreover, this white person or other non-Black serves as a foil to detract from general statements about other groups. For example, if one is explaining the potential damaging effects that Chinese immigration will have for Afrikan countries, someone will remark, "Well, all Chinese can't be bad, because Antoine's wife Xiao Mei is a really nice and helpful woman." They will say, "It's not all whites because Becky is funny, kind, and a really good mother." Regardless of the fact that these statements are ludicrous because we are dealing with power relations between groups of people—not individuals, they serve to limit the corrective and constructive actions that families can take to reconstruct the Afrikan psyche and community at large which will eventually end in the creation of strong nations with strong national identities. Dr. Amos Wilson correctly observed that, "you have never seen multi-racial nations rise to power in the affairs of the world, you have only seen ethnic nations do this"[11] In fact, even where an exception can be made to this principle, the multiethnic/racial composition usually displays itself at the period initiating the decline in the power of that nation as we see in the USA today. Moreover, even if there are small ethnic enclaves within a generally homogenous nation, the group who is in control of the institutions and therefore the power of that nation is from one ethnic group only. Saudi Arabia is a great example of this where white Arabs control a nation with lots of non-Arab Muslims. The other non-Arab/non-Saudi Arabians have no chance of ever rising to the level of wielding the real power in the country. Whites typically engage in sexual relations and procreation with Blacks to limit the possibility of creating this essential foundation for power and seed a confused mixed-race person within the race to cause confusion and display inherently divided loyalties whenever the tendency for organizing for power should come to the fore in political discourse among Afrikans.

Moreover, whites and other non-Afrikans who sleep with or marry Afrikans usually don't have a general familiarity, love, or regard, for Afrikan people in general. They spend the majority of their time with the person whom they are sexing and tolerate at best their other family members whenever they must be present at family functions. They often ignore or do not relate well to other Afrikan people and this is why we see the phenomenon of whites and other non-Afrikans sleeping with Black people, but then seen on video or accused of physically harming other Black people, or mistreating them in some way which is racially motivated[12]. I submit that these whites and other non-Blacks have unresolved psychological issues which they are using quisling Blacks to help soothe. They typically feel inferior in relations to other whites and want to feel a sense of domination over someone who merely wants them because they are white. I have had the occasion to hear whites openly confess that they chose a non-white lover or mate (in these cases it was an Asian or mestizo) because this object of their desire only likes white men and so he (the white person) does not have to work as hard to attain their affection or be satisfied in the relationship. I am sure all of us have had the occasion to be on dating websites for one reason or another and seen an Asian, Black, or mestizo woman state that they only want white men to respond to their profile posts. Unless it is a Black woman with a race consciousness or a degenerate white woman, you will never commonly see a request that only Black men respond to these advertisements. Both white men and women know that they have this value in the IR dating market, so if for some reason they do not find satisfaction in the ethnic white community where they are from, they will look for a fawning sycophant from the non-white world. It just stands to reason that the rejection or dissatisfaction the white person has experienced in their own community will have a negative psychological effect on them as a person. They then go and hunt for a non-white mate to satisfy this distorted desire they have and commonly cause damage to the psyche of the Afrikan or other non-white with whom they mate, especially if they have kids with that person.

Another motivation is the attainment of the prize negro. This typically happens with celebrities, be they sports, music, or movie stars. Whites and other non-Blacks also see these people as safe, and the Afrikan chosen is usually apolitical and/or liberal. Any political activity is done with the approval of whites and for the cause that they champion only. Even if an Afrikan celebrity is helping Afrikans, they are doing so in a safe area where whites do not feel the development of power will occur by their assistance. These include anything to do with HIV/AIDS, building schools (which often teach a Eurocentric curriculum), "empowering women" (whatever that means), or something with the environment. However, whites search for these Blacks and manipulate them into thinking that mating with a white will show other Blacks that the world is moving forward towards a post-racial and eventual raceless society. But their intent is more sinister I think. By Afrikans, who have attained monetary success within the white-controlled economic system, or by participation with it, subsequently mating with non-Afrikans, they reduce the possibility of building intergenerational wealth for Afrikan people. They reduce the possibility of creating children who will not only carry on the legacy of the founder of that wealth, but start other ventures and developmental projects to be beneficial for Afrikan nations. Think of Michael Jackson's white kids. The creation of intergenerational wealth is one important factor in how whites developed their powerful nations through families like the Rockefellers, the Astors, the DuPonts, and the Vanderbilts. It would be difficult for me to name an Afrikan family with this type of intergenerational lineage and impact. Furthermore, by producing a hybrid kid, they permanently damage the genetic line which produced the talented Afrikan person in the first place. In rare cases, the mulatto may display some of the characteristics of the Afrikan parent, but it is not common and highly improbable. Even if they do, the hybrid will have a tepid relationship with Afrikan people generally. The damage this does to the psyche of normal, everyday Afrikans is severe. People take the example set by the Afrikan celebrity as the ideal mode of behavior. They confuse the success the Afrikan person has attained in the white-dominated economic system to infer that this Afrikan person is actually intelligent about <u>ALL</u> things, and therefore his or her behavior should be emulated. The white or non-Afrikan in this case has no regard or involvement in real and pressing issues that Afrikan people face and succeeds in drawing the successful Afrikan away from involvement in these issues as well, if the desire was even there in the first place.

Other non-white people will date Afrikans to escape their own homogenous cultures because they feel they want to be unique or seen as "worldly" by sleeping with, marrying, or mating with a negro. The Afrikan person usually has a deep and untreated sexually fetish that was likely started by the unremitting addiction to watching pornography. They want to experience sex with the object of some of the videos they have watched and hence find common ground with a non-white, non-Afrikan person who also wants to escape. These relationships do not usually last long, especially after the kids arrive. One or the other individual realizes that their fantasy was just that, *a fantasy*, and they flee to a more stable setting. However, the damage is often not able to be undone, and there exists an Afrikan with hybrid children from a misguided, ill-fated, sexual affair that they attempted to bring into reality. Others, simply want to be fashionable and show that they too are part of the white-generated idea of "progress"[13] by mating with someone from the Afrikan race. They think that Afrikan genetics are meaningless and therefore if they have a hybrid kid that they call Black, and use the kid to create more confusion in the Afrikan societies, it is just a normal occurrence in the long march of progress towards the "one world society". These people are indifferent to what Afrikans actually want or need and have taken the liberty of projecting their own rancid beliefs onto a powerless people

62

to accept. Non-white, non-Afrikans would never accept a hybrid to be in power in their own societies and they know that others of their society would not accept them as such either. So, they are using Afrikans societies as a test laboratory for their crackpot sociopolitical theories. Willing Afrikans go along with this who are hypnotized by humanism, Marxism, and other dead-end theories created by non-Afrikans for how the world should be organized and how Afrikans should look and behave in it. The fact that we have not updated our own intellectual tradition has left us vulnerable to ideas which are constructed with the intention, whether implicit or explicit, of wiping us from the face of the earth. This is why any ideology Afrikans adopt and develop must be based on who we actually are, and not faddish creations by people with deep and abiding sexually-driven psychoses.

In summation, it is not likely that the white or other non-Afrikan person that one chooses to mate with can bring anything of value to Afrikan people. They often present more damaging possibilities than anything that can be construed as an advance from an **ACBN** point of view. These people predominately have psychological problems and should be avoided at all costs by Afrikan people when choosing a mate. I often ask the following question to people who seem to believe the answer to their love life lies outside of the Afrikan race. If one is unsatisfied by continuously experiencing a series of failed relationships with non-Afrikan people, and one thinks that Afrikan people are also unable to satisfy one's desires for intimate partnership, then what is the difference in having multiple failed relationships with white/non-Afrikan people and multiple failed relationships with Afrikan people? The answer... *the hybrid kid.*

The congenital biogenetic confusion of the hybrid

I have talked about something I refer to as the psycho-history in this book. Psycho-history is a term used by some writers on political theory and history. I first came across the term when reading Dr. Amos N. Wilson books[14]. My understanding of the term is that psycho-history is the group psychology which develops in a racial group of people based on their distinctive historical experiences *as a race of people* which makes an indelible cultural and genetic imprint that is then passed down through language and behavior to a succeeding generation. It is not easily changed, but can be expanded with new national experiences of trauma, success, and other spiritual or intellectual movements. From this understanding, it is clear to me that Afrikans, Asians, Europeans, Arabs, and other groups of mixed-race individuals like mestizos and the groups who make up populations of south Asia have different *psycho-histories*. These psycho-histories manifest in behavioral tendencies among individuals of that race that cannot simply or perpetually be undone, but can be masked or manipulated from time to time. Several books have been published about the cultural, intellectual and psychological histories of these groups. For example, Dr. Marimba Ani examines European culture from an Afrikan-centered point of view in her seminal work, *"Yurugu"*. Dr. Chinweizu, Dr. Amos N. Wilson and Dr. Kobi Kambon discuss Afrikan psychology in their books, *"Decolonizing the African Mind"* (Chinweizu)[15], *Black on Black Violence"* (Wilson)[16] and *"The African Psychology in America"* (Kambon)[17]. I am sure there are other books written about other groups of which I am unaware, but I am certain that they contain this element that I refer to as *psycho-history*. In fact, all literature is little more than the retelling of the psychology of a people. By literature, I mean prose, poems, fables, fairy tales, jokes, oral histories, songs, dramatic literature (plays, television shows, movies), graphic literature (comic books, videos, visual art), legal, philosophical, or political treatises, history, and academic writing produced to inform or explore a topic in detail. If the creators of literature are especially manipulative, the psychology of a people can be distorted to induce new behaviors and worldviews, but this is ultimately damaging to a people if it is not commensurate with their genetically infused psycho-history. For instance, war propaganda has this aim. If leaflets are dropped, as some nations at war have done, to persuade the enemy it is in their best interest not to fight because the aggressor will be more lenient if they do not resist, then this is a form of manipulating psychology to induce a certain behavior which may not be in the best interest of the group, or even related to what the target group is engaged in fighting to defend. Another example is by producing copious literature, you can convince a group to accept and even practice behavior alien to its culture, like homosexuality. However, just like the nation under direct attack at war, if the ideas in the literature are accepted by the target group in contravention to its historically created psychology to know what is best for group survival and health, eventually the group's population will dwindle, disease will increase, and it will start to accept other perversions which might lead to its internal decay, downfall, or its invasion by another group. However, the point is not that psychology is reflected in a people's literary output per se, but that people maintain access to their psycho-history through such. There are details in literature that resonate on a deeper plane of human existence, be it emotional or spiritual, when we see it depicted in literature. This is always specific to particular groups, notwithstanding that certain ideas in literature are also pervasive to the general human condition.

I wrote the proceeding passage to establish a foundation for why two people from two different races, with two different psycho-histories, forged in isolation for thousands of years in different geographic regions, with two distinctively different genetics, cannot produce an offspring which can be genuinely representative of either group. Of course, the individual offspring might be healthy and a successful individual, but I am talking about this with respect to *the group*. The combative and adversarial relationship of Afrikan and non-Afrikans, particularly the European whites in recent centuries, has created a power imbalance which renders any procreative sexual interaction damaging to the group with less power. People frankly do not want to admit that the hybrid kid belongs to neither one, nor the other racial group, and not least due to the fact of the competition for self-actualization between the two sets of genetic contributions within the individual hybrid itself. This creates a congenital (from birth) confusion in the identity of the individual who must, out of primal necessity, find acceptance not just among the hybrid's parents, but among the kith, kin, and ultimately the racial group of both parents. White people, in order to correct for this natural disparity in the self-perception of the hybrid (and themselves), long ago created categories of mixed-race people and rules such as the "one-drop rule" (hypodescent rule) to designate the kid as either non-white, or part of the Afrikan race. Due to the fact that the kid knows that he or she has a white parent, it also knows that it is not completely Black, since it obviously cannot be completely accepted as white. This in addition to the competing psycho-histories which relegate one parent to a racial underclass and the other to the dominate class. This basic confusion about its place in human biology _and_ a racially-tiered culture can only be rendered meaningless if the kid makes one of two decisions. (1) The hybrid decides to partake in the racial society of the non-Afrikan parent...meaning that the kid assumes the view that he or she is a human (read: *white person*) *"who just happens to be"* part Black. (2) The kid accepts his membership in the Afrikan group, but as a "Black" person with a white parent, meaning the person maintains some part of his or her **essential, biogenetic being** within the antagonistic white racial group that in part created him or her. "Biogenetic" means the genetically manifested biology of the individual; the genetics providing the design of the individual's biological form and shape within physical existence. Quite often, both decisions in their own way, but particularly decision (2), result in a psychology that in part admits the dominance of the white parent's racial group and the acceptance of such dominance by other Afrikans. The acceptance typifies the perverted attention of what are erroneously called "light-skinned, Black people" (again, a contradiction in terms) as being the most desirable sexual mates within the Afrikan racial collective. Moreover, the occupation of these mixed-race individuals in positions of power and influence over the Afrikan collective insure that the hybrid's white parent's group maintains dominance over Afrikans via proxy. If the leadership of Afrikans is by a **non-Afrikan**, be they a white, Arab, Asian or a mixed-race person (a non-Afrikan person with one white or other non-Afrikan parent) then the subjugation of Afrikans continues under the supposed, self-serving and servile, magnanimity of "not being like our oppressors". The magnanimity is expressed by the act of not rejecting someone from our group based on race. However, while the oppressors _are successful_ in their socially and legally codified rules of social interaction concerning who is in the group and who is not, Afrikans have not been. So, is the fleeting moral victory of not being exclusive really the correct tactic to use for achieving the political victories we claim that we desire?

For those who accept the term *"colorism"*, I add the following essay for your consideration which approximates my views on the issue.

The following section is from taken from the blog "The Lumumba Afrika Report"[18]:

> *"The European not only colonized the world, but he colonized knowledge and knowledge of the world. He even colonized the image of god!"*

> *~Dr. John Henrik Clark*

The above quote is one of my favorites from Professor John Henrik Clarke because in it, he is basically saying that if Afrikans are to regain any sort of power, we have to start to define knowledge and the concepts that the knowledge describes or refers to in our own terms, especially when using European languages. The more correct term I'd like to offer for consideration is *Lightskinism.*

Lightskinism is the occurrence of mixed-race people demanding that Afrikans acquiesce to them being actual biogenetic Afrikans because IMAs (Inbred Mutant Albinos are Eurasian peoples, particularly western European whites) have said so or because they are a conscious mixed-race person. Furthermore, it's a disposition that demands Afrikans treat them with deference and/or adoration or it is the deference and/or adoration of mixed race people by Afrikans over and above actual biogenetically Afrikan people. We often see this in the area of "Black leaders" in some Afrikan continental nations, and the expatriate colonial states like the USA, who are frequently mixed-race individuals and not Afrikan. This is also particularly operable in beauty standards and sexual relations as Afrikans seek to emulate mixed-race (and white) people by skin lightening and buying fake hair. However, and most importantly, it is the sexual fetish and fascination Afrikan males (and increasingly some Afrikan females) have specifically for mixed race women/men in an effort to produce more hybrids through procreation so that there will be more in existence to soothe their shattered egos due to the reality that they are Afrikan without industrial, military, economic, and political power like other major world groups. Hence the only recourse is to attain a fleeting genetic power and the reverence for having had sex with or producing a mixed-race person. This is presently referred to as *"colorism"*, but the term *"colorism"* doesn't go far enough to explain the phenomenon. This is mainly because some mixed-race people claim that Afrikans are "colorist" towards "light skinned Blacks" (mixed race non-Afrikans). This is similar to the charge of reverse racism issued by IMAs. The charge is baseless in both cases because both groups are actively seeking to keep Afrikans powerless on a widespread scale. However, most Afrikans care little to nothing about attaining power over these other groups. Hence it should be correctly termed, "lightskinism", not colorism.

To return to the topic of this section concerning the biogenetic confusion of the hybrid, I would like to conclude the discussion of the implications of the genetic melding of two dissimilar psycho-histories within one person. There is a third decision the hybrid can make regarding its basic confusion about its place in human biology and a racially-stratified culture which has arisen for hybrids recently. That is to become the stateless, internationally *sophisticated*, "global citizen". (*Sophisticated* in this case refers to its original meaning, which is <u>to tamper with, to disguise, to make less natural, or to trick with words; to quibble or use sophistry</u>. The usage here is **not** the more modern meaning of being stylish, cultured, or educated.) This is the person who has accepted the fashionable propaganda of there being an emerging global society which will eventually be raceless in nature and will focus on *"the content of people's character and not the color of their skin"*[19]. This tragically-hip milieu includes people from all racial groups and mixed lineages, but it is not the majority of people on the globe by any means. These types of people are usually concentrated in the major metropolises of the west, which have an inordinate amount of presence in globally projected corporate media content to present these people as being on the cutting edge of a new type of human society. I had the occasion to meet many of these such individuals and they have some interesting views on reality. One Asian person mentioned to me that if they start handing out the *"global citizen card"*, she wants to be the first in line. This regardless of the fact that it is still only physically possible for a human to be at one place at one time, so what would possibly be the benefit of having a global citizenship card other than to assist in the ability of organized power groups to track people and catalogue her activities? Others are more aware of the political division in the global order, but still think the solution is for everyone to love each other more by breaking down barriers, borders, and eliminating "old ways of thinking", which in their minds is anything which limits their ability to have no responsibility to any definable group of people anywhere, except to the amorphous concept of "humanity". Others still think that it is an untenable and volatile geopolitical situation, and the best solution for them individually is to be the lone hybrid (or person of pure racial stock) living as an "expatriate" in another group's homogenous nation so as not to arouse too much suspicion. The goal is to be a novelty for the enjoyment and interest of the local social misfits who want to attain any distinction that they can from their fellow countrymen without actually having to give up participation as a biogenetic member of their homogenous society and being a primary beneficiary of it. One such account of a hybrid who has chosen the third way is in the following essay:

Taken from the blog "The Lumumba Afrika Report"[20]

> I overheard a conversation recently between a mulatto acquaintance of mine and another Black man which revealed something very interesting about the unintended results of interracial breeding and the impact it has on mulattos.

The mulatto was asked if he was going home to visit his family for an upcoming vacation and disclosed that he was not. The reason he gave is that when he visits his home it is not the same anymore because most of his childhood friends are married now and staying in his parents' home is not an option due to their lack of interest in him.

He was pressed on his meaning of this final point and he subsequently revealed that his parents were perfectly willing to meet him in a restaurant for a meal and hear about details of his life, but as far as staying with his parents for the duration of his vacation time home, he was certain that could not occur.

Again, he was questioned as to why this was and he disclosed that his biological parents are actually divorced now. This was a bit of information that I did not know, but had suspected since I know that these tragic arrangements (interracial marriages) don't usually work out. His mother is African and was born on the continent and his father is an IMA (inbred mutant albino) AKA white.

He said that some years ago his father had remarried a white hippie woman and that she was a university instructor and very "liberal". She was into all this LGBTQ-LMNOP stuff and during an alleged nonchalant conversation had baited him into a trap of admitting that he did not really care about the political result of such matters one way or the other. At the time, the mulatto was 20 years old and was just not interested in whether homosexuals had or had not rights. This is quite a normal view of people his age. But this "liberal" immediately ran to the mulatto's father in tears claiming that he had horrible discriminatory beliefs and she was afraid of him and so on. The mulatto's father backed up his new white wife and literally told his son that "She is my wife now and you have to accept it and her beliefs". The mulatto later rightly suspected that this hippie wanted to marginalize the white man's children from the previous marriage and succeeded in setting him up in a fake row so that she could justify the father's decision to limit contact with him, which he ultimately did.

In an ironic, but not too surprising twist, the African mother of this mulatto is living in an all-Black neighborhood in the USA which is wrought with all of the stereotypical ills we have come to associate with inner-city living—single mother culture, limited worldview, lowered expectations, lack of social courtesies, and reduced income potentials. This is turns out is the reason this mulatto is living far from home and continues to seek out opportunities that restrict his ability to return there.

After hearing the story, I found it astonishing yet typical, and not all too surprising, that this is the result of these interactions. The faux liberal white male (or female) is commonly looking to fulfill a fantasy or desire for the world to reflect their half-baked ideology, and so he mates with an Afrikan woman in order to satisfy some need or solve a perceived social problem which only he can do because of his "white male capability and compassion". However, the social problem which is attempted to be solved through this behavior is never resolved and is only exacerbated. The outcome is that the white participant gets tired of their negro pet and the race-based incompatibility of the relationship rises to the forefront. I suspect that as time goes on, often the white partner (especially the male) realizes that the social capital they lose by marrying a negro and having mulatto children is not sufficiently balanced by their satisfaction in strictly adhering to their ideological tenants. So, in this case the IMA male divorced the negro and found an IMA (white) wife in order to regain some of his lost manhood and respect in the eyes of his white compatriots. This is why he mentioned to the mulatto son that "this is my new wife now" in an effort to establish his new social reality in the mind of his mulatto son and limit his access to him in certain social situations. Moreover, because his son does not look like him, he had to, in a very passive-aggressive way, impress upon his mind that any experiences he will have because he is not a white person should not be brought to the doorstep of him and his new white wife. This resulted in the mulatto creating a life for himself elsewhere and pursuing not only non-Black females, but non-white

71

female romantic partners as well. The likely product of his life, should he choose to procreate, will be another mixed-race person. The child will be either mixed with Asian, or Arab, or some other female from a mixed-race group like mestizos.

The African mother who fought so hard to disavow her Afrikanity and possibly dreamed of a lavish lifestyle in the arms of her "rich" white man from the west, ended up terminating herself genetically and living among the very Africans that she was trying so hard to escape.

These liberal whites mate with Africans and other non-whites usually due to a sense of powerlessness in their own socio-political structure and want to feel some power, *any power*, by offering the fantasy of social uplift into *unattainable whiteness* to some non-white sycophant. Reality creeps in eventually, and the white person, reticent to give up their "liberal" delusions, then makes the unconscious decision to reject the pet and her children and marry a white hippie who would protect his cover of being "non-racist" and interested in social justice, while he can safely and without negative repercussions reject his bastard offspring from his ill-fated, sexual, social experiment. Luckily for them, the white legal system has defined his children as Black, so he is comfortably assured that he has no further responsibility for the outcome of their lives.

My conclusion and moral from this story…DON'T RACE MIX! It doesn't solve the problems you intend it to solve and it invariably just causes more! There is no ultimate benefit to anything in this behavior but to your loins in such unions. The misplaced value that Africans place on pale-skin is a death warrant to your race and your own personal genetics. The mulatto children will quietly resent the position you put them in of being stuck between two worlds. That is being rejected by racist anti-Black parent and embarrassed about their self-loathing negro parent who hated themselves so much that they were compelled to produce a genetic mutant.

The hybrid can never really go against either side fully, or to state it more explicitly, they can never go against the group which has more power. On one occasion, I was privy to a conversation with a mulatto who was sharing an incident where he was talking to another non-white man he had happened to meet. The man was not Afrikan, but nonetheless, non-white. The non-white man was expressing his dislike for white people and for some reason felt comfortable about giving his opinions about them to this mulatto stranger. Now, it could be the fact that the non-white individual did not know that the mulatto had a white parent, but what was more interesting was the reaction to this disclosure the mulatto gave to the non-white man. The mulatto told me that during the rant he was trying to interject statements like, "Oh white people can't be so bad, don't you remember that little white girl you had a crush on in elementary school?" He said this in an attempt to get him to retract some of his views on whites and when he didn't, he said to the non-white man, "What about those white guys you played soccer with in high school, do you hate them too?" Now mind you, the mulatto had no knowledge of whether either of the above incidents ever happened, and he was relaying the story to me as if he was trying to talk down a crazed person intent on committing some violence against whites, which the man wasn't. In my view, I think the mulatto actually thought that I would agree with him for diffusing the other non-white man's anger. However, I, as an Afrikan man, just thought that the mulatto was protecting his white parent's group of people and image against a clear-headed victim of global white-terror domination, although I did not say so at the time. In fact, in an interesting irony, just that morning a totally different non-white man of the same ethnicity as the man "ranting" mentioned to me of his dislike of whites for having colonized Afrika and that, in his opinion, Afrika would be in a much better developed position now if the Europeans had not have gone in and stolen all of our wealth. I agreed wholeheartedly with him with no second thought. He went on to say to me that he does not like the arrogance of white men and tries his best to avoid them when he can. Again, I made no attempt to defend whites, and naturally agreed with this person's position. It goes to show that due to having been sired or birthed by a white person, something within the very genetic makeup of the mulatto cannot accept the total revulsion felt by clear thinking non-white victims against one of their parents group. The above situation is similar to the occasions when Afrikan people hear so-called "liberal" whites, whom we think are our friends and like and respect us, make jokes about Afrikan people or use a racial epithet and think it's okay, or if we are desperate to remain "cool" in their eyes we will laugh. However, the sinking feeling or overt disgust that we have for that white person is nevertheless felt, even if we put on an accommodating smile for them due to fear or necessity to keep a job. We have the same sinking feeling and revulsion in our biogenetic being, and it is no different for the offspring of a white person when protecting their parent's people.

People underestimate the power of DNA because we do not understand that DNA is our biogenetic inheritance from all of our ancestors; which is a physical manifestation of how they evolved from time immemorial. DNA is transmitted to us through our parents and most of our DNA is directly from them, so this means that if someone is mixed, (even if they are "cool") they will always have a fundamental confusion about their very biogenetic existence, *and not necessarily their social existence*. This is where we as Afrikan people are confused. The different genetic lines, as well as the psychological histories of the peoples associated with the two different DNAs, are perpetually competing for self-actualization. In the long run, it is a fight the mixed person is bound to lose. The results of this lost battle by the mixed individual usually negatively affect the group from which they come who has the least power or knowledge of self. In today's world, this is the Afrikan group. □

Why mulattoes and other hybrids are not Afrikan

Taken from the blog "The Lumumba Afrika Report"[21]

When I first became aware of this issue, it took me a year to finally accept this conclusion. I had an argument with a YouTuber concerning this issue in reference to a video he posted entitled "Just because you got black in you." He proceeded to say that racially mixed people (i.e. people with parents from two distinctly different racial groups with one being Black/Afrikan) are not Afrikan and I predictably had an emotional argument referencing the systematic rape that occurred to Afrikans perpetrated by whites (Europeans) in the USA which resulted in the wider spectrum of skin color seen in the Afrikan population in the US today. However, after failing to convince him and unsubscribing from his channel, I had several months to listen to interviews and read a lot of material, historical, biological, sociological, and political. I eventually reached the conclusion that indeed he is correct. Hybridized people are not Afrikan and should not be accepted as such.

Before you throw around the term "racist", let me define the term as per my understanding. The terms "racism" and "racist" are actually misnomers. The phenomena should more accurately be termed "ethnocentric economic protectionism for the purposes of seeking, securing and wielding wealth and power". Understandably, with this more accurate term, it is more convenient for the "racists" to use the former terminology because it deftly conceals the true nature of the phenomenon and makes confused, naive, and unsuspecting people believe that "anyone can be racist" because they treat someone of another race or more appropriately termed "geno-cultural group" (Baruti, 2006), rudely or make disparaging comments about them. Moreover, the more academically accepted terms "white supremacists" and "white supremacy" are actually not correct terms either, although from a Eurocentric point of view these terms do surreptitiously stimulate the "utamaroho" (Ani, 1994), of Europeans and people classified as white, these terms are nevertheless used to describe the phenomenon in critical race theory and other fields of study. The appropriate terms are actually either "white world domination by terror" (Kambon, 2006) or "white hegemony". This is an ideology that holds that whites are better, smarter, and more capable producers and managers of wealth than non-white people, and specifically those categorized as black. Hence it justifies by any means necessary the total destruction of any successful model of development independent of whites or without white people leading, organizing and directing it. The logic of this racial hierarchical model proceeds downward with each racial group being more adept at this activity than the lower caste. This ideology informs the system of "white supremacy" that is presently masquerading as globalism. Therefore, it is impossible for a non-white victim (and especially Afrikans) of this system to be a racist, practice racism, be a white supremacist, white hegemonist, or participate in white ethnocentric economic protectionism or "white world domination by terror" in any way that ultimately benefits his or her existence within his or her geno-cultural group and the group as a whole entity as such.

So back to why mulattoes are not Afrikan. Firstly, I would like to posit the view that mulattoes are genome terminator entities, meaning that they can't reproduce themselves like their respective parents can if they had have mated with one of their own geno-cultural group. A mulatto must mate with another mulatto to reproduce themselves or else their offspring reverts back towards whichever geno-cultural group they have chosen to mate with or they create another hybridized offspring should they decide to mate with another hybridized person or someone from a geno-cultural group which is not one of their parents. Hence their genome pattern cannot maintain structural integrity and they terminate. This is actually the strongest argument for why mulattoes are not Afrikan. Every other geno-cultural group on the planet knows this including the hybridized groups such as the Arabs. The Hispanic/Latinos are another matter which I will address later. I won't discuss the Indians of South Asia (see the talk by Dr. Velu Annamalai – "Dali: The Black Untouchables of India" on YouTube) but one could reasonably compare my discussion below of the Hispanic/Latinos with that of the Indians, although it is not entirely the same. Other geno-cultural groups never accept a hybrid as one of them. This DOES NOT mean that they treat the hybrid unkindly or should do so in all cases, nor does it mean that the hybrid cannot participate in economic or educational opportunities. However, at the level of strategic power in which the lives and destiny of the geno-cultural group are at stake, hybrids have no place, no relevant voice in matters such as these as they are not part of the geno-cultural group's GENETIC survival. This is an error that Afrikan people have made. They have assumed that because of "racist" practices of other geno-cultural groups to cast off their hybrids among us, even when they have been created but not fully accepted among the ranks of others, and furthermore the other groups made rules about why they have done so, (i.e. the one drop rule), we have felt an obligation to accept them which has resulted in a non-exclusive preachment befalling the Afrikan geno-cultural group. This failure to address who is Afrikan and who is not has left us vulnerable to infiltration, not only by hybrids, but by non-Afrikans under the false claim that they are too Afrikan because they were either born on the Afrikan continent, they have some distant ancestor who participated in or was raped into producing a hybrid, or they cling to an as yet unproven theory of the "out of Afrika hypothesis" of human origin founded with the propagation of Darwin's THEORY of evolution. This has left Afrikan people without a codified set of standards, rules and regulations about who is an Afrikan and has exposed us to confused mulattoes seeking a constituency and other unscrupulous interlopers seeking to dominate us. It was part of racist practices of our enemies to create a one-drop rule. White men did it so they wouldn't have to legally and formally acknowledge the offspring they had as a result of raping Afrikan women and mulattoes. Whites and other non-Afrikan groups, but especially Europeans demand that their hybrid children identify as Afrikan and not as a member of the other parent's geno-cultural group. This is inherently racist because they do so to maintain the purity of their own geno-cultural group to the detriment and pollution of the Afrikan geno-cultural group. Whether or not mulattoes can build a coherent geno-cultural is the problem of their white and negro parentage, and since their white parentage presently have more power, the responsibility primarily falls to them.

In fact, I would submit that non-Afrikans who pursue sexual relations with Afrikan people are practicing ethnocentric economic protectionism by way of furthering the social hegemonic aspect of this system, albeit it in a vulgar, perverted, and insidiously biologically destructive way. These people know full well that at present Afrikan people are the least respected geno-cultural group on the planet, so they are seeking to fulfill a need to feel superior to someone through a sexual encounter (which is one of the most vulnerable situations, psychologically and spiritually, a victim of this assault can engage in) which is done most likely due to a sense of inferiority in the non-Afrikan's own geno-cultural group, or the perpetrators are inherently lustful and perverted and seek to satisfy carnal sexual fetishes at the expense of the non-geno-cultural other, in this case the Afrikan.

The Afrikan geno-cultural group is under no obligation through this behavior to "accept" mulatto offspring as part of our geno-cultural group any more than other geno-cultures. It is due to our relative powerlessness and refusal to strictly define who is an Afrikan that has led to this confusion. Afrikans as part of our liberation and industrial renaissance of Afrikan civilization, must codify and institutionalize a valid definition of who is an Afrikan. I would suggest reading Chinweizu's discussion of the "mirror test" for some insight into this matter (Chinweizu, 2006).

Now concerning the so-called Hispanics or Latinos. The term Hispanic simply means a person who speaks Spanish. It is not a racial classification. Therefore, since Spain is in Europe, Hispanics are primarily European white people. The victims of the conquistadors, who were forced to speak the language are largely the remnants of the indigenous nations which were extant in the Americas prior to invasion from Europe. There has been massive hybridization due to the forced rape practiced by the Europeans and the voluntary rape that results from having been conquered wherein both women and men seek to relate in an intimate way with the geno-cultural group that represents power and control in the imposed society. Latino is a Spanish word that means Latin. Latin is another now defunct language that was spoken in Europe. So, the two terms to refer to this group are European languages in origin which have nothing to do with the heritage culture of the preponderance of people in the Americas that these terms indicate. Latin or Latino is used because that was the language of the political theological institution (the Catholic Church) used to repress the minds and cultural rituals of the victims of the colonial enterprise in order to make a more docile population able to be exploited efficiently. Detractors or rebels of the theological doctrine were tortured or killed, so this created a fervent adherence to the religion closely intertwined with one's own survival which we still see presently. Today in this population, since those people who speak Spanish in the Americas are from various origins (i.e. Afrika, Europe, and indigenous American nations), it cannot be said that these people are a distinct race. In fact, the archetypical "Latino" or "Hispanic" is actually a hybridized person who is conditioned in a false consciousness to identify with the colonial culture that was cultivated by European settler-conquerors. Within this group there are still enclaves that have retained their indigenous language and cultural practices, but for racist reasons they are labeled as "Latino/Hispanic" to again stimulate the utamaroho of the European descendants and immigrants that are interspersed in this population, so that they feel a sense of comfort knowing that the language still reflects their own worldview and identity. The majority of the hybrids in this population are victims, and some have reproduced to the degree that they can be considered a distinct geno-cultural group or race, but they have not as yet organized themselves in such a manner mainly because they are still prisoners of the European colonial social construct. Additionally, given the imperial reliance on their economic activity as a source for raw materials, cheap labor, and consumption markets, they are victimized economically and therefore cannot undertake the necessary steps to develop themselves in this way. Moreover, they still have confused Afrikans (who are descendants of enslaved Afrikans and are still repressed by both the hybrids, and Europeans) suffering from a false consciousness within their midst, as well as Europeans that are desperately trying to maintain their colonial relationship and keep enact their white hegemonist system of exploitation. Therefore, the people known as "Hispanic/Latinos" contain people on the spectrum of hybridized individuals, culturally mis-oriented Afrikans, indigenous nationals, and criminal Europeans attempting to persist in the maintenance of the monstrosity they have created.

On the other hand, the Arabs have been able to organize themselves into a geno-cultural group. This was largely done 1400 years ago through the development of their own political theological institution known as Islam which is simply Arab Christianity (Popp, 2010). Even though there are hybrids contained in the Arab population, they are either historical hybrids produced in antiquity when these white groups invaded Kemet (Egypt) and created offspring with Afrikan women, or they are offspring of the degenerate Arabs that have kidnapped Afrikan women in the present era and used them for their perverted pleasure as sex slaves. The hybrids they create are used to oppress Afrikans in Afrika and promote the expansion of Arab nationalism (i.e. Islam), even though these hybrids are repressed and discriminated as not really being Arabs themselves. It is a psychological phenomenon that is a result of both hybridization and power relationships being enforced by the Arabs on their Black Afrikan victims which compels the hybrids' fealty to the white Arab dominators. The hybrids see the true Afrikans as powerless so even though they are mistreated by their fathers' geno-cultural group, they feel the power that is available and the superior social and economic position they have as Arab identified hybrids, gives them the motivation to mistreat the Afrikans in a brutal way for their fathers' people. So, since these two groups, the Arabs and Hispanic/Latinos, are organized for white power and whites have used sexual predatory practices to attack their victims and consolidate their control, it does not mean that the hybrids are white, nor does it mean that their non-white status is a basis of solidarity with Afrikans. This is a MAJOR historical point that Afrikans have missed, refuse to accept, or have been deliberately mis-educated from knowing. The multiplicity of these factors has brought about the MASSIVE confusion about this matter. The subject is so sensitive that to even broach the topic with many Afrikans will result in emotional outbursts and vicious name-calling instead of calm deliberation and effective implementation of the proper provisions that would protect Afrikans from being used as the world's sexual toilet and dumping ground.

Lastly, and this is a radical position, I don't think that Afrikans and Europeans, or for that matter other geno-cultural groups, are the same "species". Now before you levy a charge of "Eugenics", I am arguing that the criteria and hence the definition of "THE human species" is incorrect and specifically culturally derived from European culturally structured thought (Ani, 1994) to serve political purposes and a quest for power. One of the main criterion for Europeans arguing that now (after several previous theories about the sub-human status of Afrikans and other races) humans are one species and there is "no such thing as race" is that different geno-cultural groups or these "non-existent races" can breed with one another, hence if two biological entities can procreate together it supports the likelihood that they are part of the same species, whereas if two biological entities cannot breed, for example a cat and a bird, then they are two different species. This notion is absolutely absurd. I think far too much emphasis has been placed on the breeding criterion and fact that whites and blacks for instance can have hybrid children and therefore, there is no difference other than skin color between us and subsequently, we should then "not see color" and accept all as human. This directive notwithstanding, in the Afrikan worldview and traditional Afrikan societies, Afrikans never posited the idea that people were "born human". Human beings had to be developed through education and socialization, and upon successful completion of this process, then the status of human was imparted upon an individual within the Afrikan socio-cultural context. (Baruti, 2002, 2003, 2006, 2009) It was not simply bestowed because one was born of a homo sapiens male and female. This is a distinct difference that exposes the cultural nature of Europeans' scientific classification and purposes. Basically, I am arguing that Afrikans, Europeans, Asians, Amerindians, and other hybridized people constitute different species (or sub-species) of the human "family". The word "family" in this sense is of a biological grouping, not the emotionally laden image of mom and hugs from your grandmother that the colloquial use of the term "family" generates. I am not arguing for some "shiny happy people" view of humans on earth or that we should all start holding hands and be blind to the different interests of these geno-cultural groups and their different destinies. It is quite obvious that the Amerindian nation of North America had a decidedly different destiny than say the "Sinic" East Asians, so I purport that this fact is still present today, although hidden under universalist and globalist rhetoric. The main point is that if two species or types of humans from two separate and distinct geno-cultural groups procreate, it stands to logic that the offspring is neither one or the other geno-cultural group, and thereby constitutes a new geno-cultural entity that must proceed to either develop a cohesive group with other hybrids, or must "disappear" back into one or the other parent's geno-cultural group. Azania and its "coloured" (hybrid) population is a stark example of this phenomenon, as are the Arabs and Hispanic/Latinos, although to a lesser degree, that I mentioned before. Nevertheless, I will not take time now to argue whether or not the Afrikan parentage of humanity is valid, but suffice it to say that the present definitive difference in geno-cultures will remain until one or more are exterminated by another (which I am not advocating, but is nonetheless a possibility). So, under these conditions, for Afrikans to help promote and accelerate this process by claiming that all hybrids with one Afrikan parent are Afrikan and are not either a separate geno-cultural group, or are not Afrikan and are part of the other parent's geno-cultural group, (because hopefully at some point we will have the consciousness and power of definition to codify and implement this idea into reality) is a recipe for extinction and assisted genocide.

References:

Ani, Marimba. (1994) *Yurugu: An Afrikan-centered critique of European cultural thought and behavior.* Washington D.C.: Nkonimfo Publications.

Annamalai, V. (c. 1994) *Dalit: The Black untouchables of India.* New Jersey: Afrikan Echoes. Retrieved from www.youtube.com/Afrikanliberation.

Baruti, Mwalimu K. B. (2002). *The sex imperative.* Atlanta: Akoben House.

Baruti, Mwalimu K. B. (2003). *Homosexuality and the effeminization of Afrikan males.* Atlanta: Akoben House.

Baruti, Mwalimu K. B. (2006). *Eureason.* Atlanta: Akoben House.

Baruti, Mwalimu K. B. (2009). *Yurugu's eunuchs.* Atlanta: Akoben House.

Chinweizu, I. (2006) *Self-reparation for Afrikan power: Pan Africanism and Black consciousness.* Accra: Paper Presented at The Global Pan Afrikan Conference on Reparations and Repatriation Conference. Retrieved from www.abibitumikasa.com.

Kambon, Kamau. (2006). *The declaration of Dr. Kamau Kambon.* Raleigh: Blacknificient Books.

Kambon, Kobi. (2003). *Cultural misorientation.* Tallahassee: Nubian Nation

Popp, V. (2010) The early history of Islam, following inscriptional and numismatic testimony. In K.H. Ohlig, & G.R. Puin (Eds.), *The hidden origins of Islam.* (pp. 17-124) Amherst: Prometheus Books

Chapter 3: ACBN: A Socio-Political Theory

"The Black Social Theory determines the destiny of a people by establishing guidelines of life. It defines their relationship with other living things, it defines values and rituals, methods of education, and how enemies are dealt with, etc."[1]

~Dr. Bobby E. Wright

"The most practical thing you can have is a good theory...is a good concept, to guide your behavior. To be used as an instrument to measure reality; a good theory then organizes the world and organizes one's approach to the world...it permits one to be able to evaluate the world in terms of where one wants to go and what one wants to do. To be without theory then is to approach the world on an *ad hoc* basis...always to be overwhelmed by events and overwhelmed by the future instead of creating events and creating the future."[2]

~Dr. Amos N. Wilson

Need for a Socio-Political Theory and how ACBN fulfills it

I had occasion to listen to a Black man who had converted to Sunni Islam give his opinion about an interracial marriage once. The marriage was between a British man and a Nigerian woman. This ginger-haired Brit had converted to Islam and married this Afrikan woman which had befuddled his Arab Muslim "brothers". The Black man said that when whites convert to Islam they often marry an Afrikan woman and that Arabs are puzzled by this because they don't understand why a white man would marry a Black woman. Especially, a woman whom Arabs view as less than desirable than other women who are available to most white men; not to mention the fact that most white Arabs secretly and/or openly lust after white European women themselves. He then stated that this is a case of "racism" on the part of his Arab Muslim "brothers". I remained quiet during his exposition, but I couldn't help thinking..."*Why would a Black man willingly convert to a _racist_ religion like Islam?*"

84

Obviously, I was personally disgusted with hearing about this pleasure-seeking, culture bandit taking an Afrikan woman for his wife and playing at being Muslim for whichever sick reason he had in his diseased mind. The Black man I referred to above even said that Arabs think white men are "crazy" for doing this. Well, if a stopped clock can be right twice a day, I guess that shallow Arab Muslims can be lucid in their perceptions from time to time as well.

I recount this story to lay the basis for my discussion in this chapter about the need for a social-political theory that is detached from ideologies developed foreign to the Afrikan psycho-history and moreover which are developed by foreigners who seek to exploit the minds and perceptions of Afrikans for their own political purposes. Afrikans have played with various hair-brained schemes such as communism, socialism, liberalism, Christianity, Islam, globalism, humanism, new ageism, Judaism, and all sort of other silly thought forms, religions, and political theories devoid of any specificity for the Afrikan mind, body, and spirit. They have not directly addressed the problems that *Afrikan people actually confront* and thus served as a foundation for thought and behavior which will assist us in navigating a world beset with traps, foils, and dangers designed by our enemies to ensnare us in their elaborate plans for dominating us. After slavery ended, many of us ran to the Christianity of the Europeans thinking that this religious doctrine would provide the moral framework and spiritual redemption for us to heal from centuries of trauma inflicted on us by the same Europeans. After a few of us awoke from the Christian spell, we became angry at having been duped and converted to Islam thinking that "it was the original religion of the Black man"[3]. We thought that adopting an Arab name and accepting the militant nature of Islam as opposed to "western" religions would give us the spiritual grounding and strength to throw off the oppressors. Unfortunately, the more honest among us learned that the Arab Mohammedans (now referred to as Muslims) were the first to start enslaving Afrikans, so this turned out to be a false solution too. Some of us, giddy and brimming with pride over having attained an education in a western (European) university, thought that one of the more "sophisticated" schools of political thought such as communism, Marxism, socialism, or some other such political fad would be the answer to help organize Afrikan economies and societies in conjunction with the coming world revolution to free our proletarian brothers, sisters, and "other oppressed people" of the world to throw off the chains of the capitalist exploiter class. Some of us were a little more honest, but no less deluded, when we clung to liberalism simply because we wanted to sleep with white people. We thought that by having sex with white people and voting like they told us to vote, the other Afrikans who were not lucky enough to have a white sex-mate might eventually benefit from some of the policies the white liberals implemented. None of us thought about it, or wanted to think about it for that matter, but the problem is that most of the liberals are liars and as soon as they got into power they not only maintained, but fulfilled much more of the agenda of the "scary and racist radical right wingers", whom we thought were on "the other side of the political spectrum". In the end, it turned out that "right wing conservatives" are just the distant cousins of the whites who are liberal about their choice of sexual partners, but not necessarily about which racial group ultimately rules.

This political morass we find ourselves in currently greatly calls for a radical new approach to how we organize and define our goals. At this point in history after the formal end of chattel slavery in the west (but not in the Arab east) and the apparent end of expatriate colonialism, we need to consult our history and psychology to understand what it is we are trying to regain, and who it is exactly we are trying to save.

It is best to determine this by asking a series of questions first. Number one, why do we have so many Afrikans from the west converting to Islam? This was the case with the anecdote I wrote at the beginning of this chapter. Isn't there any functional ideology based on a Black man's Afrikanity which could serve his needs? Why are there still so many Black Christians around the world? The case is settled in many books about the process by which Afrikans converted to Christianity, and it had nothing to do with an independent desire to do so. The book "How to Make a Negro Christian"[4] by Kamau

Makesi-Tehuti provides clear detail and documentation about how white men planned to convert Afrikans to Christianity in order to prevent interpretations by Afrikan men and women of biblical verses which might support their plans for violent revolts against the white oppressor class. Walter Williams has written two books called, "The Historical Origins of Christianity" and "The Historical Origins of Islam"[5] both of which have an abundance of references and supporting data. Why are so many Afrikan men and women giving up on cohabitating with one another in serious and healthy intimate relationships? If members of other racial groups (although not a significant portion of those groups) find us sexually attractive, what is it that allows us to relate to them better than we can relate to our own natural biological counterparts? In most cases it is because we have chosen to adopt a social theory that reflects *their* desires and worldview and diminishes our own. Why haven't Afrikan people at this late date developed a functional and powerful nation-state replete with all of the industrial, technological, and cultural institutions correlate with other powerful nations of the world? What prevents Afrikan men from developing trade networks and markets within Afrika among Black nations? What prevents us from creating a large and powerful institutional informational and educational network that allows Afrikans to communicate with each other to transmit valuable and life-saving information to one another? Where is our auto industry? Shipping industry? Armaments industry? Where is our aeronautics industry and space program of any significance? Where is our powerful subcontinental nation-state on the order of Russia, China, the USA, or Iran, with the power to economically sanction other countries and markets? Where is our Hong Kong or Singapore with a well-developed and industrious economy? Where is our North Korea with enough nuclear weapons to make our enemies think twice before aggravating us? And even if they do, with the nukes at our disposal, they would have little recourse to act.

It is the view of this author that these abilities and systems are paltry or non-existent because we do not know who is Afrikan and who is not. We want to call the Palestinians our "oppressed brothers and sisters" while we run off to marry white people. We want to claim the mulatto offspring of whites as Black, (even though both whites and mulattos know full well that they are not Black) just so we can feel good about having so-called "beautiful" people in the world who are called "Black" too, and thereby live vicariously through them. We want to produce hybrid kids to impress white and Asian men about our sexual prowess. We want to buy goods and services from the Asians, Europeans, Indians, and Arabs because after all, "why should we manufacture these items when we can just buy these from them?" We want to avoid social, business, and political relationships with other Afrikans because everyone knows that "we can't do shit", meanwhile we continually get used, mistreated, and discarded by the whites and other non-Afrikans whom we unrequitedly love so much. We don't want to bother building an institutional legacy for our children and subsequent generations because we are more concerned about being the "first black" something or other in another people's culture and society. And if this isn't possible, we will make an Indian or white person the first non-Black in ours so we can show whites and others that "Look, it's okay, look we're acceptable! We don't hate you for what you've done to us". If some of us are less confused and rage against the system, we modify our rants with statements like, "It's not all white people" or "Everyone has a right to live where they want". Even while we are isolated from our own markets and prohibited from their secluded neighborhoods unless we attain the status as the _safe, negro-pet_ designation and given the individual sanction to be the living, breathing sex toy of some low-status trash from other racial groups. We still refuse to admit that individual "success" does not change the collective condition of a people, nor does it change how strangers view the individual of that group. The group must have a functional system of power to protect their group interests as well as the individual group member.

We need a socio-political theory now more than ever. One that is functional and designed for Afrikan people only. One that will lay the basis for how we relate one to the other. One that will inform our view of ourselves and people who are not Afrikan. One that will provide the logic for why Afrikan men and Afrikan women need to be exclusive about our intimate relationships and exclusive about our business and political relationships, and deal with the world in a systematic way which promotes the survival of authentic Afrikan people…which are people with a skin color from dark brown to black with Afrikan-textured hair!

Afrikan-Centered Biological Nationalism provides this system of thought for Afrikans. It is the only way forward for Afrikans at this point which gives us the ethics and basis for approaching the rebuilding of our culture to a superior, unparalleled, durable and virile condition to address the problems realistically and with clarity that threaten our biological survival on this planet. It is the only system based on the fact of **who is Afrikan and who is not**. It answers the question of **who is in the group and who is not**. These criteria implicitly inform us on whom should be our leaders, with whom we should engage in marital relations, with whom we should build businesses, where our geopolitical foundation and base of power operations are, and who should be treated as an alien/foreigner/non-Afrikan. **It better helps us to recognize traitors or those with decidedly divergent interests than ours, and it allows us to focus the building of our institutions unapologetically to serve the in-group first**. We are not "racist" in the socially derogatory sense, and we don't cower at being called that term. **We are concerned with the biological survival and power of Afrikan people** in a functional national position to set the tone for the Afrikan reality of the future. We are aiming for *true sovereignty* of Afrikan people in the areas that fundamentally matter—*territorial, economic, monetary, and legislative*—which will give us the power to build all of the attendant institutions of national organization that arise from these.

What is ACBN in terms of social, economic, and political organization?

ACBN is a socio-political creed which defines Afrikans by biological traits for the purposes of organizing a set of socioeconomic relations to achieve power for Afrikan people. ACBN relates to areas of activity within the *social, economic, political and spiritual* spheres of

Afrikan life and existence. The main purposes are to engineer a social system in which Afrikans psychologically and socially seek their primary relations with other Afrikan people for work, education, organization, recreation, and procreation. ACBN is designed to protect the genetic integrity of Afrikans and insure the genetic survival of Afrikans and the Afrikan genome as it has existed from time immemorial.

To reiterate, ACBN defines[6] an Afrikan / Black person as one who is clearly a "close" descendant of people from East Afrika, a region comprised of countries now known as Kenya, Tanzania, and Uganda. Afrikans' color variation ranges from bronze, dark reddish-brown, dark or nut brown, dark-chocolate color plus *"peppercorn"* hair. It[7] does not include people with a non-Afrikan parent or people who are living on the Afrikan continent but do not fit the above described phenotype. It does not include all of humanity based on the Darwinian theory of evolution, any other unproven theory of human origin, or the "Out of Africa" hypothesis.

Social relations

ACBN recognizes that it is the set and system of social relations inherent in a cultural civilization that defines how goods and services are exchanged, information is conveyed, and individuals are to succeed based on developing and applying their individual and collective talents within the population. ACBN recognizes that the foundation of this system must reside in building families and extended families via the institution of male and female procreative realities and capabilities. Inter-racialism, or promotion of pseudo-scientific theories such as the "one drop rule" and "Black dominant genes" are rejected. Instead, the relationship between the Afrikan man and Afrikan women within the context of the familial community and its connection to the larger society is fostered and promoted preeminently.

Furthermore, relationships within the collective for industrial productive capacity are encouraged among groups of Afrikan men distinct from groups of Afrikan women. The same is encouraged and

90

promoted for groups of Afrikan women. The youth are socialized into this reality of a division of roles with respect to one's biological functionality within one's genetically determined sex. This does not negate the need for Afrikan men and Afrikan women to work together in non-sexual industrially productive capacities as well.

Economics

ACBN recognizes that no ideology can succeed or find advocates which does not provide a material benefit to its adherents. Therefore, a practical a viable economic approach which focuses, in part, on the principles of Nguzo Saba[8] are infused throughout the programs and policies which are adopted. Economic policies are conceived from the basis of the Afrikan worldview which included collective responsibility, collective work, and collective benefit which are balanced by individual commitment, individual development, and individual accountability. Specifically, Afrikan-centered culture and warrior-hood are to be pervaded throughout the economic enterprises which sustain the material existence and comfort for Afrikan people. Expectations to reflect the values, ethics, history, aesthetics and mores of Afrikan culture are demanded and through a system of reward and punishment are reinforced in the conceptual approach to functioning in daily life. To put it simply, in the ACBN society, "you don't bite the hand that feeds you" and Afrikan people are the ones who do the feeding.

Economic policy recommendations will focus on the essential areas a civilization needs to survive such as food production, health maintenance, military, crafts, manufacturing and infrastructure building and maintenance. Strategic areas of growth will also be encouraged so that Afrikans gain control of large and essential parts of economic activity, such as software engineering, mining, aerospace engineering, communications, information technology, weapons technology, medical research, energy and transportation, and so on.

Political

ACBN, being the ideological underpinning of a socio-political economic system, does entertain (and does not discourage) the formations of schools of thought in the different areas of human activity and intellectual development. This tendency in the management of human affairs leads to the development of factions which seek to satisfy certain constituencies within the social order. Even though this phenomenon is encouraged and the subsequent sub-political formations will be integrated into the society as a whole, all such parties will be counter-revolutionary and conservative with respect to the ACBN ideology and its fundamental foundation in the Afrikan worldview. The essential social theory that provides the groundwork out of which will spring groups which both agitate for representation in the institutional network of society, and seek to have a relevant voice in the distribution of resources, will be that the genetic survival of authentic Afrikans is the basis of our system of social relations. In addition, non-Afrikans do not have a biogenetic stake in the survival of the Afrikan genome, so therefore cannot be considered relevant in the panoply of issues that naturally will arise when engaged in direct and indirect management of the power, wealth, growth, development, maintenance, and well-being of Afrikan people.

Spiritual

One of the most profound attacks on Afrikans historically was the introduction of foreign ideologies masquerading as religions onto the Afrikan psyche. Much research has been done by Afrikan-centered scholars and researchers to reclaim authentic Afrikan ancestral religions and the diverse way in which they were manifested, recorded, instituted, and practiced. It has been concluded through copious research and in voluminous publications[9] that, for Afrikans, the acceptance of foreign ideologies masquerading as religions is a violent psychological attack and jeopardizes the biogenetic survival of Afrikans both directly and indirectly. This renders the acceptance of religions which are not designed for the survival of Afrikan people rendered moot and judged by the historical record as being a material and immaterial detriment to the health of Afrikans in the mental, intellectual, and physical spheres of existence.

Therefore, since all civilizations need an ethereal thought system to undergird the conceptual superstructure of the civilization, Afrikan ancestral religions will be promoted and instituted throughout the society to address the spiritual nature of authentic Afrikan people as our ancestors had identified and codified through numerous texts, artifacts, and literature. Since all sane, self-interested geno-cultural groups enshrine the worship of their own image through the depiction of their deities and the practice of ancestral communion, this will be the fundamental spiritual approach with regard to the establishment of the major religious institutions and celebratory rituals commonly known as "holy days" or holidays which will provide the spiritual satisfaction for Afrikans in this area of human life.

ACBN incognito

One of the best things about ACBN is that it can be done individually. One can choose a spouse, friends, business relations, a career, and a place to live all to enhance one's ability to apply ACBN directives effectively without the need to consult others or to join an "ACBN group". Quite frankly, we commonly make these choices anyway, it is just that some Afrikans are compelled and feel justified in choosing non-Afrikan spaces over creating or renovating Afrikan ones. Although a person can be an Afrikan-Centered Biological Nationalist (ACBNist) in a non-wholly Afrikan environment, it is not sufficient to bring about ACBN aims. Examples of being in a non-holistic Afrikan environment and conforming to proper "*ACBN social behavior*" are being in surroundings with non-Afrikan people and choosing not to engage in activities and conversations which are counter-productive to ACBN aims. Other examples of this are praising mulattoes and other non-Afrikan women's beauty over and above the beauty of Afrikan women or not praising beautiful Afrikan women at all. Preferring the company of non-Afrikan people over the multitude of

Afrikan people who have noticeable intelligence and standards of morality are choices we can avoid. And as I mentioned before, choosing where one lives is well within the power of a person applying ACBN values, so this should be considered carefully upon the decision to practice ACBN tenets. In order to clarify what I am proposing, sometimes it is best to look at examples from foreign cultures to understand how these practices can be applied. For instance, in Arab Muslim culture, it is considered an offense to ask a man directly about his wife, even if it is merely asking about her well-being. In the Judaic religion, it is forbidden for men to shake hands with a woman. These are the kinds of *social standards* ACBNists should have. I am not suggesting to practice these particular ones per se, but some topics and forms of discussion should be seen as rude and off limits in ACBN culture, such as verbalizing adoration for non-whites with European features, following the leadership of mixed-race people or congratulating Afrikan people who are in mixed-race marriages. Others are practices such as when engaged in discussions of the political nature, we should have clear cultural guidelines like staying on topic and refraining individuals from seeking to dominate discussions simply because he or she enjoys talking (or hearing oneself talk). Social practices like these can help ACBN communities be more effective in planning and implementing policies in the places where we live. One must start these practices among individuals and/or families, then communities, and ultimately nations that are consciously and ethically living by ACBN values.

ACBN does not require that anyone joins a political party or social uplift organization specifically associated and certified by an ACBN ruling politburo. I personally feel that it is important for Afrikan people to be part of an organization of some sort, but its goals should correspond as much to ACBN goals and aims as possible. If the goals are not equivalent, then the contribution the Afrikan-Centered Biological Nationalist should make is to prod the organization along ACBN lines of thinking and policy formation. If that is not possible, then starting or joining a new organization with the proper goals in conjunction with ACBN is another possibility.

ACBN is a relatively new approach and therefore it needs more writers and thinkers producing literature. This is also a task that can be done in virtual solitude. With the rise of the Internet and online media, it is possible to publish articles, books, create visual media and make websites for a fraction of the cost of media in years past…and reach a much wider audience! This can be done in small collectives or by one person without upsetting the present organization of one's life if one is unable to make more radical changes due to current living circumstances. For people in a position to hire or award contracts and provide business to other people, using ACBN standards would help a long way in syphoning off some monetary wealth from non-Afrikan sources to help with other Afrikan organizational and industrial efforts. ACBN does not require that you stand on the street corner like a raving lunatic to get followers, nor do you have to join the lecture circuit to rouse up the amen corner, you simply must agree with the definition of who is Afrikan and then organize your tastes, values and desires accordingly to fulfill the aim of living a life which empowers Afrikan people first and foremost.

Chapter 4: America or Afrika?

Decline of America

America is in decline. There is no need for me to make the academic argument for this because the signs can be seen all around you. At the very least, the USA is undergoing fundamental and irreversible change after which the position and opportunities for the Afrikan collective will be severely reduced and we face the likelihood of ceasing to exist as distinct and recognizable group of people. The fact is that the USA has been in decline as of this writing for well over one hundred years. During that time, it has undergone significant changes to its national character, form of political organization, and the ideology of the white faction which comprises its ruling class. The ruling class has abandoned certain responsibilities towards the white body-politic for various reasons, but most notably are their desires for continued global domination over *all* nations, and their subservience to the financial and banking sector which holds an enormous debt on their stolen, wealth-generating, property[1]. The abandonment of the lower class white stratum of society by the ruling class does not mean that we are "all the same" now and are part of a multiracial fight against the ruling class or "1%". Quite the contrary. The white ruling class is not that stupid. The opportunities for upward mobility for whites may be more restricted, but the whites are given other advantages and diversions to keep them docile and complacent. One such salvo they have is their dependency on cheap prescription and illegal drugs[2]. Another is the ability to travel to exotic locations and be served by non-white servants who require their patronage to survive. Other perks are the ability to openly have sexual play with non-white sex mates, and to still be given relative power and authority over Afrikan people via seemingly innocuous jobs and positions such as office manager, school teacher, police officer, prison guards, and other menial management positions in retail stores and other service industries[3]. If the white person is somewhat scholarly and ambitious so that he or she attains a post-graduate education, becoming a school administrator, city official, judge, project director for a research firm, or some other type of professional is another advantage they receive for their acquiescence to the changing America. If they are technologically inclined, trading one's knowledge and skills to serve the national security state and military-industrial complex are still viable opportunities for white men and women and here too, they have the opportunity to oversee non-whites with similar or superior skill sets. Although some are noticeably angered at their diminished prospects and the unadulterated changeover from an America viewed as majority white, to one with populations of riff-raff and scalawags from every hamlet across the globe which resulted in whites *collectively* voting to elect Donald Trump, they still have access to operating the levers of technocratic[4] control in service of the ruling class whites[5] in the USA. This is also true in the increasingly multiracial societies in Europe like the UK, France, Italy, and Germany which are also being bombarded with migrants from former colonial outposts.

The fact of the matter is that the original idea of what the USA was created to be was pretty much over after the end of the US Civil War in 1865. A lot of Afrikans are confused at this point. We often think the war was fought to free our enslaved ancestors, and to a degree it was, but the war was more about **a political dispute among two political factions of whites** who were in disagreement about how to interpret the nature of the union between semi-sovereign states. The details of this dispute are beyond the scope of this book, but suffice it to say that the USA was supposed to be a loosely confederated group of sovereign economic-states with the ability to practice their own form of economic organization; independent of one another except where two main features came into play. One was the regulation of interstate commerce which required federal courts to adjudicate and legislation to regulate, and the second was to provide for the common defense of all member states against an aggressor whether internal (Afrikans and Indians) or external (other European nations, particularly Spain and the UK). A third and less important feature was to protect the rights of individual citizens of each state which was inconsequential and virtually unnecessary if the former two features of the political agreement were followed. When this deal was abandoned by the industrial-financial north when they imposed tariffs on goods imported from England, goods which the agricultural south needed to buy to operate its plantations, an irreconcilable political rift was formed between a group which wanted to follow western Europe into the finance-industrial form of economic organization, and a group which wanted to retain the original constitutional agreement and practice an agrarian-patriarchal economic organization. Well, we know who won the war, but I do not think Afrikans to this day really understand what the implications of this was for us living in this foreign political system and socio-economic culture. The fact is, according to Euro-American legal and cultural viewpoints, with which both the northern faction and the southern faction agree, to have a non-assimilated, non-white (alien) group in their midst is tantamount to having a foreign occupier (albeit without the force of arms) in one's land with the potential for socio-political disruption. The answer from the south was to impose apartheid (called "Jim Crow' laws or segregation) and the answer from the north was "social integration"—which really meant _disintegration_ of the nascent, yet foreign, nation made up of intergenerational Afrikan _prisoners of war_ within the territorial borders of the USA.

Due to the colonial beginnings of the USA, the republic was always more susceptible to influence from elements inimical to maintaining its European cultural origins. Not "European culture" in terms of racial stock, but in _European political form_. The fact is that the USA was started as a haphazard attempt to seize land and wealth from non-whites without any overarching plan except to just gain more wealth. This tendency, as history has shown, resulted in the ruling classes perpetually being amenable to schemes and ideas to increase its economic prowess, even if it was poisonous to its founding documents and original political arrangement of the first 13 states. Therefore, with the passage of the Federal Reserve Act[6] of 1913, the moneyed class (a class of people in the financial sector whose business is the creation of money through the issuance of debt instruments) were able to take control of the policy-formation process and legislative control of the USA without the ability of the group who wanted to keep the founding charter of the United States (the

98

constitution) intact and applicable, able to prevent them. This has led to the disastrous social and political experiments of the 20th century. It also resulted in the ability of this moneyed class to fund various degenerate social and artistic movements like the Civil Rights Movement (really Consumer Rights), Hollywoodism, Teenage (youth) culture, Feminism, Post-Modernism, Homosexual Rights, Suffrage Movements, Internationalism, Humanitarian War, Pornography, as well as many others, and in addition, but no less detrimental, the change in the form of social interaction and entertainment from community-based to home-based in the form of print tabloids, television, radio, and the Internet.

The point of this passage is to say the Afrikans really need to think long and hard about how we are to attain political power in such a system which has all but disenfranchised its white constituents from participation, except as an overseer class to non-white inhabitants and immigrants. I often hear politically active Afrikans repeat the rhetoric contained in the constitution or other laws (which were written out of convenience by whites) in an effort to browbeat the whites into enforcing them to our benefit. This is the height of naiveté and quite embarrassing given the real political divisions in the country and the traveling road show which is thrust upon a demoralized public every four years in the form of "national" elections. Afrikans think that voting an Afrikan man or woman (or even a non-Afrikan who is "on our payroll") into one of these offices is going to give us bargaining power to arrest some concessions from the system. It might work in the short run, but the concessions we really need are actually an existential threat to the continuance of the system, so we could never be the ultimate winners by operating by that approach. Afrikans are under the illusion that *politics* consists of joining a political party, lobbying a legislator, running for office, or voting. These activities are not politics. These activities are merely the practice of participating in somewhat organized gangs to fight by various means for economic benefits from a governmental system whose reason for being is self-perpetuation and self-enrichment in the service of the ruling plutocrats. *Politics*, in the strictest sense, is a national organization of people who have an indelible and distinctive culture, and whose natural hierarchy and social organization supports every institution in the nation for the biological survival of the people contained therein. This form of politics always has a definable territory, always maintains control over strategic resources and infrastructure for the national benefit, always trains its youth and the more capable members of its aristocracy for the proper handling and management of power in its essential institutions, and *always, always, always* **has enemies** who want to prevent the nation from doing this; thereby necessitating a strong and effective military to protect it physically, economically, and psychologically from attack. Everything other than this is *ANARCHY* –plain and simple. I do not mean the "romantic" form of anarchy often espoused by rebellious youth in which it is proclaimed that "*no one can tell me what to do*". Nor do I mean the more refined adult version in which it is asserted that you are an "*individual, doing your own thing*". I mean the form of anarchy where the strongest gang gets the spoils and if you are not part of the strangest gang you are a slave, or at the very least an insignificant cultural critic on the outer bounds of society satisfying one's carnal desires which is justified by a self-serving ideology of individualism and one's membership in an amorphous and abstract concept called "*humanity*". This is not what Afrikan people need. It is not what ACBN promotes.

To be perfectly blunt, I am endorsing Afrikan-Centered Biological Nationalism to promote a project for authentic Afrikans to build a sub-continental "Black Power" nation-state in Afrika with economic outposts in the Afrikan diaspora which can positively impact the sociopolitical-economic realities and destinies of Afrikan people[7]. The hybrids can develop whatever system they think will solve their existential problems. Whether it is to continue selling themselves to Europeans as an international buffer class for the oppression of Afrikans, or to establish an internationally recognized identity of their own. I am only concerned with achieving and maintaining authentic Afrikan power for authentic Afrikan people.

Can Afrikans' gain power in the USA?

Being that our main goal is the acquisition of power for a group of committed Afrikans, if an individual resides in a European expatriate colonial state, we need to ask if *real political power* can feasibly be acquired in these regions by Afrikans. Dr. Amos Wilson discusses several forms of power in his magnum opus, *Blueprint for Black Power*[8] which outlines the qualities of thinking and structures of organization necessary to facilitate a group gaining power in a particular polity. I will review a few here.

Force as power: Power as force involves the exercise of biological and physical means to prevent another person or group from doing what he or it prefers to do; inhibiting or destroying another person's or group's ability to develop and mobilize his or its human and material resources which might be used against a foe.

Coercion as power: The instrumental use of force or the threatened use of force by the power holder to attain the compliance of another.

Influence as power: Occurs when a person acts in compliance with the wishes, directions, or suggestions of another based on his sheer positive regard of love or admiration for the other or based on a desire to please or serve the other because of the other's personal significance.

Competency as power: The achievement and exercise of social power derived from knowledge and skill and where behavioral compliance is obtained from the subject in return for his receipt of some benefit or service awarded by the authority.

Legitimate authority as power: A power relation in which the power holder possesses an acknowledged right to command and the subject an acknowledged obligation to obey.

Manipulation as power: The attempt by the manipulator to elicit certain desired responses from the subject while concealing his efforts to do so; it is more efficient than force, coercion, or influence because it is less likely to evoke resistance since the subject is unaware of the manipulator's efforts to influence him or may think the results are desired by both the manipulator and the subject.

Social power: The possession or control of some important or valued material and/or social resource which is the basis of power. By strategically rewarding or depriving others of these resources, one may influence behavior in ways compatible with one's interests.

Property and power: Confirms an economic power which gives the power holder the ability to decide what will be produced, how much it will cost, how many people will be employed, what their wages will be, what the price of goods and services will be, what profits will be made, how these profits will be distributed, and how fast the economy will grow.

Organized networks and power: The systematic channeling and distribution of energy or force along definite pathways in order to achieve some definite outcome. Organization imposes direction on otherwise random, relatively diffuse, unfocused, or erratic phenomena in order to generate a focused, concentrated form of power directed toward accomplishing particular goals.

Collective power: This is enhanced and stabilized in a social group to the degree that its control is institutionally based on commonly accepted values, rules, laws, and norms. Cultures and societies normally achieve their routine goals through institutionalizing much of their social behavior and activities by founding and operating institutions designed to organize social behaviors and attitudes towards the accomplishment of certain tasks.

Ethnic solidarity and power: Power formed by a group sharing among its members a common history, set of values, fate, plight, or on their consciousness of (having) a shared collective identity. These shared factors form the basis of a group solidarity and the use of solidarity to generate and exercise social power.

Amos Wilson writes, "The crucial importance of ethnic identity or solidarity and social organization among (the) Afrikan (Americans) [*Parentheses added*] and their relationship to that community's ability to exercise extensive and intensive, authoritative and diffused power in order to successfully counter its domination by the White (American) [*Parentheses added*] community, underlies the White community's unceasing efforts to atomize the Black community into a mere aggregate of disunited individuals—individuals lacking or weak in social solidarity and organization."

Dr. Wilson then quotes the following from Horton and Hunt (1968) "The struggle for power often appears to be largely a contest between organizations...the power of highly organized groups is only checked by the opposition of other groups."

First to clarify the direct quote from Dr. Wilson, in my view it would be better to read the quote as, "social organization among Afrikans" and "domination by Whites" rather than adding the adjective "American" to the group designation because my particular book is intended for Afrikans in Afrika and in the Afrikan diaspora.

Now, onto the discussion of why I included these snippets from Dr. Wilson's master work "*Blueprint for Black Power*". If Afrikans are to attain power in any of the European expatriate colonial states including the USA, Canada, Brazil, the remnant colonial states in the Caribbean, or the metropoles in Europe like the UK or France, we have to understand and come to terms with these forms of power. We have to assess which are the most potentially available to us, and which of these do we have presently. I included the quote referenced by Dr. Wilson because I want to stress that *this planet is operated by groups*! It is not operated by "all of humanity" or is it trending towards that end. It is certainly not operated by individuals. So, claiming that one is an unaffected individual trying to accomplish individual goals is absurd. Even if one thinks that, the alleged "individual" is operating within a social system created, controlled, and maintained by a definable group of people which has real power over the ability of the individual to participate in that social system. Therefore, if Afrikan people are to attain power in the USA or any other expatriate colonial state, we must be an organized group.

Otherwise we will simply be powerless individuals engaged in the process of satisfying personal vices.

I now turn to Dr. Wilson's descriptions of organized networks, collective, and ethnic solidarity as power. In these three descriptions, he implies three main features contained in each, although separately they each have their own particular distinctions:

a. Organized direction and management of energy to achieve a goal
b. Commonly accepted values, rules, laws, and norms
c. Members have a common history, set of values, fate, plight, or shared collective identity

These are essential in the foundation of a power group. Without these features as a foundation, it is near impossible to accomplish the goals of a group wishing to wield any sort of effective power in the social environment. I argue, based on the recognition by Dr. Wilson of "the White community's unceasing efforts to atomize the Black community into a mere aggregate of disunited individuals— individuals lacking or weak in social solidarity and organization", that the likely outcome of continual hybridization and acceptance of hybrids into the Afrikan collective as full members and *more importantly leaders* who set the agenda for the activity of Afrikan people **has** *and* **will** continue to undermine the potentiality of obtaining these basic forms of power. If Afrikans have no commonly accepted values, rules, laws, and norms such that anyone can be Afrikan, it fosters more unnecessary confusion and limits our ability to obtain power. If any Afrikan in an interracial relationship, or any hybrid offspring of a misguided Afrikan—an Afrikan mind you who *has chosen* to make one of the most important decisions in one's life that one can, that is the choice of a non-Afrikan mate with whom to create new life on the planet—is allowed to participate in the Afrikan group, without any circumspection or standards imposed by the group, **then this poses a major existential threat to the biological survival and psychological identity of the group**. This keeps us in the trap of whites attempting to keep us disunited, with divided loyalties, lacking in discipline, and a maintaining only a tenuous adherence to social solidarity and organization; not least of which is refusing to accept norms of <u>who is actually Black!</u> Very often the trap is set and administered by *poorer and lower-class whites* whom we think and say are being oppressed by rich whites too, but in actual fact, they simply have few prospects for power within the white collective, so they exert the limited social power of *white skin,* over the powerless and gullible members of the Afrikan group. Mixed-race people do not have a common history as Afrikans and they do not have a shared identity. They may be mistreated in some way by their white family members, but that does not mean they do not have a white lineage which also shares a history with other whites. Authentic Afrikans do not have this. Authentic Afrikans also do not have a white parent *by genetic connection,* nor other white family members *by genetic connection,* whose relationship with us jeopardizes our ability to act jealously for Afrikan group interests. This is why the power groups we create should first be based on who is Afrikan. Then through institutionalized organization, other laws, norms and values will be created with the goal of achieving power. At present in the European colonial expatriate states, authentic Afrikans with sexual fetishes for non-Afrikans, and non-Afrikans attempting to intercede in Afrikan affairs, present a real challenge to effectively organizing to attain *real political power* in these areas.

Next, since I used the term *"real political power"*, I would like to briefly examine what that entails. I will use the other descriptions of power offered by Dr. Amos Wilson of property and power, social power, and manipulation as power. These three forms of power also have certain implications which make them somewhat interrelated. According to my understanding they are the following elements:

    a. The exclusive possession of strategic resources by the group or key members of the group.

    b. The ability to control the manufacture and distribution of these resources.

    c. The ability to train professionals to provide services associated with the management of these resources.

Having these elements in addition to the foundations of group power I mentioned earlier, provide the framework for obtaining what I called *"real political power"*. This is power by an organized group with similar values, norms, and laws which govern the social interaction of its members, control the access to key resources (including territory); resources that members both within the group and outside of the group need to function in their daily lives. The power of manipulation relates to property and social power by having essential control of some form of information, media, or communication infrastructure that transmits messages members within the group need to know, and information members outside of the group ***should believe*** in order to fashion their behavior according to the in-group's interests. Dr. Marimba Ani in her seminal masterpiece, *"Yurugu"*[9] has referred to this as the *rhetorical ethic* which is indelible to European culture and thought, but it is nonetheless an effective tool for *inter-group relations* and has been amazingly successful in Europe's rampage over the globe these last few centuries.

Lastly, the five remaining forms of power which I listed from Dr. Wilson's book are both effective internally and externally as ways to exercise *real political power*. These forms of power are <u>legitimacy</u>, <u>competency</u>, <u>influence</u>, <u>coercion</u>, and <u>force</u>. In terms of legitimacy and competency, these are the forms of power Afrikans desperately need within the collective. Having mixed-race leaders negates the legitimacy power that they can have over Afrikan people as well as the potentiality of being recognized as legitimate power by external groups. If Afrikans continue to allow the ascension of hybrids to a leadership position, our enemies can rest assured the we are not only still confused about who is Afrikan, but it will allow infiltrators both white and non-white to seep into or communities and societies and exploit the weak-minded members into implementing their will and nefarious plans for our continued disorganization. For example, "Sweet Micky", the homosexual lifestyle promoting mulatto, and Prime Minister of Haiti from 2011-2016, who was funded and supported by Bill and Hillary Clinton through the Clinton Foundation, was easily accessible and amenable to the wishes of his white extended family members in his and their efforts to destroy the people

106

and economic potential of Haiti.[10] He facilitated the entry of multiple NGOs and multinational corporations to exploit the natural resources of Haiti at the expense of the Haitian-Afrikans. He had no compunction about doing this, not least of which is due to the fact that he is not a biogenetic Afrikan.

As far as competency and influence, these are too very advantageous forms of power to exercise political power both internally and externally. Competency relies on having a network of educational institutions under complete Afrikan control, which train members of the group to rise to positions of power based on (1) having successfully completed the formal training in the institution, and (2) undergone some period of apprenticeship to those who hold power in the group currently. This competency must be validated by material proofs and tangible accomplishments in the real world which then bolsters the legitimacy of the leadership among others in the group. Influence can take various forms. It can be the influence of an exceptionally talented person in convincing others in the group of a proper course of strategy to pursue, or it can be the influence of a recognized elder whose life work has demonstrated the capability to move the group forward to attain more power.

Coercion and force obviously are the most inefficient forms of power since they take the most direct energy to apply. However, they are critical to the internal policing and military protection of the group. These forms of power are usually shared between interrelated institutions such as research institutes, media outlets, industrial manufacturing, educational institutes, and the formal organization of ranks of soldiers, sailors, airmen, and a loyal and internally trained officer class. The application of direct force by those who hold the power in intelligence, policy-planning, and military institutions, work together to enforce the group's *real political power* against external foes, and ensure internal cohesion remains effective.

Before I conclude this section, I would like to say a word about rich Afrikan people and their relation to power. Often times we hear people lament rich Afrikans for what they are not doing to help

Afrikan people collectively. Some criticisms are warranted and some are probably just venting anger over various socio-economic issues we face as nationally and geopolitically oppressed individuals. Some people say rich Black people should be doing more to help other Black people by starting business to give Black people jobs. Some critics of this view say it is not possible to only hire Black people in the colonial states of the west because the Black business owners will be seen as practicing "*reverse racism*". Others say if rich Black people help other Blacks, the white power structure will commandeer their wealth because "white supremacy is global" and there is no escape. However, regardless of how valid these statements may or may not be, I would like to address the specific point of having Afrikan-owned companies hiring all Afrikan people in the form of a corporation. Now whether or not this is possible is not so much the issue (I happen to think it is possible), but what I think *is* the issue is the implication of the statements. Namely, that rich white people start companies and hire predominately white people, as well as some non-whites who have skills that some whites do not possess, or that white corporations can get more cheaply, so if we follow the logical implications, that means that rich Black people will need to hire non-Afrikans in their companies too, in order to compensate for the lack of desirable skills that Afrikans have to offer or in order to be more competitive in the marketplace by keeping payroll costs low. These assumptions that we cannot have anything all Black otherwise the whites will attack us, or that we must mimic white business practices to be successful, are not all together accurate if the structures of organization among the Afrikan group are done appropriately. I do not particularly think that rich Black people are in a position to help us, even if they wanted to (which I don't think they do), while there is no political consciousness among Afrikan people. Simply having a corporation owned by a Black person who hires other Blacks actually will not solve our problems. The problem we have <u>is political</u> in nature and <u>requires a political solution</u> along the lines of what I described politics as really being about in the previous section called "Decline of America". For example, in a nation like South Korea, there are rich Koreans who start businesses and hire only Koreans. If they need a worker with a specialized skill that no Korean person has, they will contract a foreign employee for a period of time to fill the position. However, as part of the contract, it is either explicitly expressed or implied that a transfer of knowledge will occur from the skilled foreigner to the Korean national. This is perfectly logical, and according to the natural exchange of services and knowledge for monetary compensation, it should not be too antithetical to the short-term goals of the skilled foreign worker. But the reason the Koreans can do this is because they have a political entity known as the Republic of South Korea which gives them sovereign control over how they organize their business practices and resource distribution through the exchange of labor for salaries. Each person in the business concern has a political consciousness of who is Korean and how this is associated with behaving in the culture. Now that is not to say there are no problems in Korean society, but they can obviously more easily address these issues with these types of organizational structures under their direct control. If businesses were to be started with a political intent to empower Afrikans in the expatriate colonial states of the west, the above example is the sort of tactic which must be employed to achieve the strategic aims of group empowerment. Specifically, using the resources of others to our collective advantage and surreptitiously, or openly, transferring the resource to our direct control. However, before this can occur, both the rich Black person and the other Afrikan participants must have the proper Afrikan consciousness of the political necessity to do this and a working knowledge of who is in the group and who is not. Without these traits, any business started by rich Black people will ultimately only benefit whites, and more than likely be taken over by whites who _do_ have a political consciousness[11].

To illustrate this point, I will relay the following historical incident. When the first white settlers started to land on the shores of the Americas and Afrika, they took with them a political consciousness which informed them of who was in the group and who was not, in other words they knew who was white/European/Christian, and who was not. Of course, some of the whites adopted the culture and ways of the Indian people who were in North America when they arrived, but they were inconsequential to the European project for power which continued unabated despite these wayward few who found solace, opportunity, and comfort in alien camps. However, a white person abandoning the group does not preclude their political consciousness from being awakened and called upon in service of the group. One such example is Kit Carson[12]. Kit Carson spent around 20 years living with Indian people in the North American continent. He learned their languages, learned the skills they had developed to survive, and had attained an intimate knowledge of the wilderness, culture, and environment where these people lived. When time passed, and the Europeans had the need to seize the land of the Indians for expansion, they commissioned Kit Carson as an officer in their military and he served as an intelligence agent basically revealing the secrets, ways, and culture of the people who had trained and befriended him for almost two decades. He had no compunction about returning to his actual political group. This is what power does for people who recognize it and are aware of the political organization which is endemic to their biogenetic being. If we are all people and "race doesn't matter", why didn't Kit Carson work for the Indians who helped him survive all of those years to defeat the marauding whites? Because it was more appropriate for him to align with the group aiming to attain power and who shares his identity as well. All of those years in the wilderness did not wash away his core identity and allegiance. Incidentally, Kit Carson married two different Indian women and had one kid each with them. The marriages did not last though. One ended briefly after a year or so, and the other wife died. Out of the two kids total he had with each of these Indian women, the one kid who survived into adulthood did not interact with people from her mother's family and nation at all. In fact, she felt no allegiance to these people and was raised in Saint Louis, MO. These marriages and mixed offspring were of no use to save Indian people from the onslaught of the Europeans. So, there was ultimately no benefit to the Indian women marrying this white man for the Indian group's survival. This perfectly summates my description of the reasoning and motivations behind these relationships that I explained in Chapter 2. However, for Blacks, who have been separated from a true political organization and consciousness, we think that participating in organizations with alien races is an end in itself. In general, we do not have the political consciousness which will positively affect an organization of biogenetically similar individuals to work together for power. We would rather accept fleeting trinkets and perceived advantages offered by an alien group in exchange for turning a blind eye to the destruction of the group. Now, I think Kit Carson's actions against the Indians was reprehensible, but I respect his group solidarity with his geno-culture when the time came to achieve power. Quite frankly, I too would rather have one Afrikan who has the character of Kit Carson on my team, than a group of Afrikans the size of an Indian nation unconsciously helping an enemy in their midst.

Consequently, unless there is a committed and skilled group of Afrikans from all income and social strata who have a political consciousness with the intent to attain *real political power*, and the wherewithal to recognize who is Afrikan, and who is not, in my humble view, there will be no achievement of group power in America or any other expatriate colonial state in which you happen to reside.

The case for Afrika and repatriation

Having established the unlikelihood of an Afrikan group obtaining real political power in the foreseeable future in the expatriate European colonial states or metropoles of Europe, I would like to turn to Afrika as a destination for a group of Afrikans who want to work together for the achievement of real political power in local, regional, continental Afrikan, and global affairs.

The attraction as Afrika as an area for ACBN practitioners to do this socio-political-economic-spiritual work is ideal for several reasons. First of all, there is an abundance of affordable arable land for purchase. Afrika is actually largely underpopulated in relation to its size[13] at present, and this makes available plenty of space for buying plots of land to build houses, communities, manufacturing plants, technological infrastructure, and to start many other businesses. This requires a person with an enterprising spirit and a viable plan in order to accomplish it. However, if this is not you, buying a house or land on which to build a house in an urban environment is also an option in many Afrikan nations, and for a far cheaper price than one would pay in the west. This of course would still require one to have a plan as to how one will earn income after the initial investment for a living arrangement is made.

There are also apartments for rent for rather cheap prices in communities of friendly neighbors located in urban settings which could provide an abode during the transitional period when one is looking for the appropriate permanent place to settle or buy land for a long-term dwelling. Having a home base is key to starting the essential work ACBNists must do to retreat from the pressures, frustrations and responsibilities associated with building the necessary social relations and organizations to facilitate our move into a power position. So, I would advise not to take this decision lightly and do one's due diligence to ensure that the people with whom one is dealing are reputable and trustworthy. I would suggest making at least one or more trips to the area or areas one is considering to relocate to meet prospective partners and other repatriates who might be able to help you with traversing the business culture and negotiate with sellers. Doing the proper research is important here because if one moves rashly without much thought, it is likely that one will have to return to the USA very soon and become crestfallen and discouraged with the possibilities of Afrika as a destination for this activity.

Another key factor in the attraction of Afrika is the fact that there are active sociopolitical groupings with existing membership and infrastructure already located in Afrikan nations. Becoming an active participant in one of these groupings with an agenda which might be molded over time to conjoin with ACBN goals is a real possibility, and it is a necessity, if we are to start to reconnect with Afrikans on the continent and help them to benefit from our knowledge and experience gained in the west. We definitely need politically-minded people on the ground who are aware of the dangers to our biological survival which the items I have outlined in this book represent. In addition to this, the opportunity exists to start a totally new organization using the latest techniques of mass communication and marketing to disseminate the message of ACBN to those with the skill, intelligence, and interest to act on this knowledge. Again, techniques discussed in the section "ACBN Incognito" may be useful here to the person with a pioneering personality.

Continuing and Community Education is something which is severely underdeveloped in many Afrikan nations and monetizing the delivery of such through offering various classes for practical skills in conjunction with classes teaching cultural, historical, and political awareness might generate the income and community involvement necessary to start to expand the depth and breadth of outlook some Afrikans already have. Many of us Afrikans have had education and training to gain essential skills, but these skills need to be spread and transferred throughout the entire populous of Afrikans globally if we are to see real change in our situation from that of passive acceptance of our situation, to one which has the will to empower ourselves to fulfill our collective destiny as Afrikan people. Chief among these essential skills are linguistic skills for the purposes of translating various Afrikan standard literary works for speakers of the multitude of languages indigenous to Afrikan people. Others important skills are health and medical, computer and technology, organizational and management expertise. These types of skills should be infused throughout the general population so the most capable among us can compete for the creation of new ideas, technology, and have the ability to manage the expansion and diffusion of the most successful creations of the Afrikan world for our benefit. We need to be the arbiters of our creations and cross-apply these from one Afrikan nation to the other without interference from alien groups seeking to implement their agendas for global dominance and management at our expense. If we have a strong and committed group or groups in Afrika taking the responsibility of this upon ourselves, we can at least mount a viable effort to reclaim our birthright in Afrika. This does not in any way leave out those who choose to stay in the diaspora. We will certainly need a business, economic, and cultural connection with them too. However, we should all start to realize that our geopolitical center should be in a strong Afrikan nation or group of nations.

Often people make excuses for not repatriating to Afrika and some are valid, yet most are not. The major excuses range from claiming that Afrikans do not like members of the original diaspora taken during **The Black Chattelization War of 1442-1888** (*aka* Trans-Atlantic System of Black Chattel slavery)[14] _to_ claiming that one cannot survive in Afrika because it too backwards and poor. Of course, we know Afrika has many nations and areas within which to live and the images that are constantly streamed on media outlets does little to give an accurate picture of the possibilities there. If they did, people from every group on the planet would not be going there to vacation, relocate, and start business ventures. If Afrika is an impossible place to live, why are millions of Chinese, Arabs, Indians, and Europeans flocking there every year? And if they are doing it, why aren't we, the children of Afrika, taking the same plunge?

The simple fact is that a person can live a very comfortable and productive live in Afrika if one does what I suggested and visit before relocating and then make a *realistic plan* for how to survive once one is settled there. There are several opportunities to thrive, more than I could possibly name here. I am also sure there are many new ways one could become innovative in how the manner of life is lived in Afrika once the children of Afrika taken for enslavement are *in country* and interacting with fellow Afrikans. Personally, during my visits to the continent, I did not experience an abundance of negative attitudes from other Afrikans, actually the opposite was true. At times, I had to literally hide from some of my friends because they were demanding too much of my time and attention to participate in Afrikan cultural functions, and I could not attend to my personal work. Of course, not every single interaction was positive, but where on earth is anyone going to experience 100% positive experiences anyway? Certainly not in the west!

One particularly valid reason people have for not leaving western nations are due to familial relations. I won't create a false impression of what moving to Afrika involves. The cost of the flight to some areas in Afrika is one of the most expensive routes to buy if coming from the west. This means that for family occasions such as weddings, reunions, and funerals, the cost to return to the west will be quite high, especially if there are multiple affairs such as these in one calendar year. Therefore, proper preparations and considerations should be made regarding these eventualities if one does decide to repatriate. However, West Afrika is the closest to the western nations and so choosing this destination might be more manageable than South, Central or East Afrika. Other considerations are age and the stage of development of one's career. These are certainly valid reasons as well, however, there are a significant and growing number of retirees from western nations choosing to repatriate to Afrika, so if one is looking to save money during retirement and experience a new environment with new relationships, Afrika presents an attractive location for this. Regarding abandoning one's career, I am sure this would be a difficult choice, so I do not want to specifically advocate for that in this section. Still, I would like to provide you with a thought you may not have considered. One of the reasons the western nations have maintained their preeminent role in economic and political affairs is due to the fact that they have large populations of individuals contributing the time and energy of their individual lives to the maintenance and growth of their societies. As long as this is the case, the imbalance in the time and energy given to growing and maintaining Afrikan societies will still remain. Unless at some point Afrikans make a definitive break and divest from the west[15] in a reversal of historical momentum which started from Afrika to Europe, but now must go from Europe to Afrika, we will never get started in firing the ignition to rekindle Afrikan power and rebirth. At some point, Afrikans will have to go through the pain of leaving what we have known and venture out to create something new. Our ancestors had to do so against their will, but now we must be willing to do so deliberately. We must if we are to realistically fill the chasm that separates us from our current state of dependency to becoming a self-creating and world dominant people again. So, we must go forward with vigor and resolve, *and I stress*, a realistic plan for success! A few more ideas for the committed repatriate are as follows.

Viable business ideas are education as I have mentioned and starting group businesses, such as manufacturing durable and non-durable goods for local consumption. Software engineering and media production present huge opportunities in Afrikan nations because the start-up costs are relatively cheap and one can operate a business via the Internet. One also has the choice of building entirely new infrastructure and platforms for viewing media content. The limits here are only in one's imagination and level of commitment. Travel and tourism are other businesses that are open to the expatriates with partnership from local residents. Using a travel business to tap into the Afrika diaspora market could create a clientele exclusively accessible to the ACBNist. Being first to establish the proper reputation and relationships before the companies operated by aliens start to market to diasporic Afrikans seeking to return home, could lead to a windfall of revenue by cornering this market and then developing opportunities for diversifying one's business interests and investments.

However, I am aware that not everyone is business minded, so preparing oneself with essential skills to trade in the job market is an option too, however one must be aware that it is vastly more difficult to find employment in Afrikan nations than it is in the west due to the level of economic development. This is another excuse people use for not repatriating, but the problem is, Afrikan needs people with particular skills for developing an economy. Such professional credentials might be limited at this time to education, medicine, nursing, engineering (all types), marketing, and business consulting. There may be more, but these are the most vital in my view. By all means do your own research to investigate whether the skills you have currently are in demand in a particular Afrikan nation. In addition, the potential repatriate might consider working for a short time with a major company or organization (e.g. NGO) just to get one's feet on the ground. I know this seems counterproductive and counter to ACBN's aims, but after one is settled, then one can start to put down roots and separate from the seething succubus that was the means to enter the country and start to actively build viable alternatives for those who will be repatriating in the future. Hopefully, if you are a diligent and productive forerunner, others following you will not have to hold their noses and work for the enemy while laying the groundwork for an enjoyable, successful, and active life for themselves in Afrika.

Chapter 5: Conclusion

Solutions

So, what are some of the things a person can do simply in their personal life to start implementing ACBN values? Well, in my view to start is quite simple. The person who practices ACBN values should make it a personal goal and/or that of one's immediate family, to visit the Afrikan continent of our ancestors at least once in one's lifetime. This is provided one does not have the intention to live there permanently. Visiting the Afrikan continent should be done with an Afrikan-owned tour company which has a focus on culture and creating business connections and investment opportunities for Afrikans from the diaspora and those on the Afrikan continent. (A suggestion for a couple of companies to use are at the end of this section)

People who agree with the goals of ACBN should start learning an Afrikan language until they attain fluency. This should be a life goal of an Afrikan man or woman and does not stop when one gets tired or lacks speaking opportunities. The official language of ACBN is IsiZulu, however in the view of this author, any major Afrikan language can be learned which is pertinent to one's needs. For example, if one is planning to move to Uganda or Kenya, learning Kiswahili would be a good choice, if moving to West Afrika, then learning Hausa, Wolof, Twi, Ibo, Ga, or Yoruba would be a valid choice. For southern Afrika, Shona or Xhosa might be the most appropriate. The point is all Afrikans who see ACBN as a viable social-political theory for their lives in relation to Afrikan people should be learning an Afrikan language. Even though all <u>AFRIKANS LANGUAGES MATTER</u>, IsiZulu is the official language because of the militaristic nature of Zulu culture. Afrikan men need an indigenous military code to take into the fields of military science, strategy, and business. It is the infusion of the Afrikan warrior spirit into these spheres of institutional activity which will help us more clearly think and plan by using an Afrikan language to create the aggressive and resolute consciousness we need to succeed in building an authentic Afrikan reality for our wives, children and families. Afrikan men need to start seeing it as our duty to control the environments where we live and reject the thought of any group of foreign men having any power or sway in our domains. Foreign men should first feel uncomfortable and if not, they should be dealt with by using the best tactic to impress upon them the urgent need for their departure.

ACBN should value self-development in the form of gaining *relevant* education and practical skills. All people learning an Afrikan language, particularly IsiZulu, should start writing articles and other useful information which catch your interests in the language you are learning. If you do not have a blog or another way to publish your writings, available options are submitting them to or posting them on Afrikan operated websites* like:

- abibitumikasa.com
- acbnj.wordpress.com.
- amosmagazine.wordpress.com
- blackjunction.com
- blaqspot.com
- moorus.com
- sonofahset.wordpress.com (the **ACBN**: *A Primer* website)

*The listing of these websites **in no way** indicates the website's expressed or unexpressed support for this text. They are listed as a resource for the reader only.

The last web address in the list is a website I started related to this book on which people can submit articles, comments, and other items to promote ACBN values via commentaries, editorials, blogposts, fora, books, and drama. ACBNists and Afrikan people desperately need drama to assist in the psychological revitalization of the Afrikan mind, particularly concerning our intimate relationships between male and female, and parent and child. ACBNists should use the media to promote our worldview to compete with the integrationist and fake "pro-Black" hustlers so to give people a stark choice regarding how they want to live their lives as Afrikans. We will incur losses, but we should focus on the generations of Afrikans' minds we can influence to change the future to align in our direction. At this point we have no other choice.

Afrikan-Centered Biological Nationalists should focus on being in committed marital relationships with Afrikan people of the opposite sex. ACBN is pro-heterosexual and sees homosexuality as a social and psychological dysfunction. The purpose of Afrikan marriages in the view of ACBN is to establish a grounding force in our communities for each adult member and to ultimately have Afrikan children to continue the quest for Afrikan biological survival and ascendency on this planet. I will not at this time attempt to admonish people for past behavior, providing it was not an irreversible mistake, but I will say that now that information has been relayed about the damage that engaging in certain behavior can have on the identity of who is an Afrikan, I will encourage that the correct choices and behavior are promoted going forward. We should be seeking as Afrikan men to adore and endorse through our consistent behavior the image of the authentic Afrikan woman as the only mate for the ACBNist. This not only occurs by proper mate selection, but by engaging in activity that reinforces the ideal standard of Afrikan feminine beauty in our architectural, conceptual, design, and artistic creations and surroundings. The Afrikan masculine standard should be reflected also in order to communicate balance, harmony, and the required involvement of both sexes' abilities and contributions. The standard for European beauty is no doubt the pale-skinned, blue-eyed blonde. So, we should have a premier standard for Afrikan beauty as well which is based in our natural phenotype indicative of the unambiguous difference in aesthetics beauty between Afrikan women and others. We should cease to shy away from this, nor should we apologize for this. This is our reality. These are our mothers, sisters, wives, and daughters both ancient and present embodied in the eternal organic silhouette of the Afrikan woman. We should have no shame in this and should revile detractors of the elegant and life-regenerative women of the Afrikan *spirit-body*.

We are at war with for our survival with non-Afrikans in Afrikan places. These non-Afrikans are infiltrating every segment of the Black world in the same manner that Kit Carson did many decades ago. Therefore, Afrikan-Centered Biological Nationalists need to become industrialists. Whether that be in the manufacturing, research, information, or technological fields. Afrikan men need to own multinational corporations which have control of essential resources and can thereby hire other Afrikan people in life-supporting jobs to demand loyalty, as well as to condition behavior in accordance with ACBN directives. There is no substitute for the control of land and modern infrastructure in a sovereign national formation[1]. Political systems emerge at particular points in the stage and level of development in a given society. What is termed "democracy" is best suited for societies that are fully developed and functioning at a high-level of production and intellectual capacity. Now, I do not really agree that democracy is the ideal form of government for all people at all times, but for the political purposes of the west during the latter half of the 20th century, it is most likely that democracy was the form which would best serve the agenda of the plutocratic elite. However, at the stage of development Afrikans are in now. The fact is that we need something much more legitimate and authoritative. Therefore, I personally advocate for a return to aristocracy and a form of government that represents something akin to a monarchy with genetic ties to the people and land rather than a cosmopolitan elite who identify with foreigners because they have similar spending power and vacation at the same popular spots in Europe and Asia. This renewed focus on a people connection via the group is what is needed at our stage of political development now. Perhaps in the future, our situation may change and require something more representative as a form of government organization like some form of "democracy" or "socialism", but for now, I think we need the most capable, intelligent, courageous, and clear-minded thinkers and actors the Afrikan race has to offer. This type of leadership is the only kind which will have the tenacity to navigate the difficult terrain which lay ahead of us. Especially as Europe continues to degenerate and Asia gains power, we will need leadership that can see the situation for what it is and not be afraid to act intelligently and forcefully in our own interests. Anything other than this at this point will just be leading us back into enslavement of either the same masters or a new master, neither of which will be favorable to our continued genetic survival.

Health and self-defense should also be standards that are maintained by ACBNists. There is a large amount of information concerning health on various Afrikan-centered websites, so a quick internet search can reveal detailed information on health relative to one's present condition. However, we all are aware that eating lots of sugar, salt, fried foods, and processed foods limits our ability to maintain suitable health. Excessive drinking of alcohol and use of illicit and prescription drugs (including cannabis/weed/marijuana/blunts) are also ruinous of a healthy mind and body. Therefore, significantly reducing or eliminating these foods and substances from the diet is a great first step toward becoming a valuable practitioner of ACBN. Routine exercise should also be part of the lifestyle of an ACBN. This can be accomplished as cheaply as doing sit-ups and push-ups daily, and jogging a few kilometers a week. One can also accomplish this relatively easily by purchasing exercise weights or joining an exercise gym to build strength, agility, and cardiovascular endurance. I personally recommend learning an Afrikan combat science such as Capoeira or Sudanese-Afrikan wrestling. If this is not possible where one is located, the mastery of the use of a weapon is another great choice to build self-defensive skills. This is relatively easy to do by reviewing videos on the Internet and taking a few hours a week to practice, preferably with other men interested in developing such skills too. These important points of health and defense help to create a mindset that will make the accomplishment of the other solutions much easier and enhance the enjoyment and success of the other solutions as well.

The solutions I have suggested are few and there may be more solutions which exist[2], but these are the basis of being a practitioner of ACBN. I do not want to overwhelm the reader with a laundry list of tasks that one may not be able to complete at present, after all this book is *a primer*. It is the hope of this author that more writers and researchers about the science and philosophy of ACBN will come forth to increase the amount of extant literature associated with this topic. The reader may already have mastered some or all of these solutions and be seeking to go to a higher level, so I suggest considering the ideas in the section, "The Case for Afrika and Repatriation". Others may be new to this socio-political theory, so starting small with the ideas for health and self-defense may be a proper fit. Whichever it is, ACBN will only move ahead when groups of men and women begin to organize around these shared values.

*Afrikan-owned tour companies:

Africa for the Africans
(website: africafortheafricans.com)

Sankofa Journey
(website: sankofajourney.com)

*The listing of these companies **in no way** indicates expressed or unexpressed support for this text. They are a resource for the reader only.

Final thoughts

Consider the following statement from a political group in the UK:

"Momentum Black ConneXtions (MBC) is an independently, self-organized, autonomous, self-determining, Black power constituency within the network of Black people and organizations to continue the energy and enthusiasm of Jeremy Corbyn's campaign. We are committed to advancing Black power perspectives on the 10 priorities that Jeremy Corbyn has identified as his own standpoint."

MBC's definition of Black is "those who do not regard themselves as white and are not treated as being white."[3]

It is interesting in the description of the group that they used every buzzword they could to try to project a view of being separate from the control of non-Afrikan groups, except for the mental control as we will soon see. They do not say exactly to which source of "Black power" they are a constituent. However, it defies logic to believe that their self-description is accurate since (1) they are located in the metropole of one of the leading white-terror states in the world, the

UK, and (2) they are attempting to gain support for their endorsement and sponsorship of a white man (candidate for prime minister of the UK) and _his_ priorities, **not the priorities of Afrikans**. This is glaringly evident in their faulty definition of who is Afrikan.

If we consider their definition for just a moment, we will see that this _includes everyone_ and does not _exclude anyone_. Firstly, they say a "Black" person is someone who does not regard themselves as white. Well, this would include the white woman named Rachel Dolezal[4] who was revealed to be claiming herself to be "Black" and working for the National Association for the Advancement of Colored People (NAACP) in the USA at the time. She carried on this facade until both of her white parents and other family members discovered this and contradicted her claims by stating publicly that she is undoubtedly a white person. Pictures released on the Internet corroborated this. Shaun King[5], another white man working for the organization called "Black Lives Matter" was too revealed as really being a white man, even though he was masquerading as a biracial/"Black" man for the purposes of spreading the propaganda associated with the "Black Lives Matter" group. Both of these people would satisfy the first part of MBC's definition of a Black person. The second part of the definition is more troubling because in an attempt to backstop their definition by stating, "and not treated as being white", _they do not specify **who** exactly does not treat such a person as white_. As a matter of fact, before Rachel Dolezal was exposed by her own parents, many actual Black people (and multiracial people who "identify" as Black) did not treat her as white! They treated her as another "Black person". So, in a hazily constructed definition of who is Black, largely based on emotional feelings, **they have made it acceptable for white people to literally be viewed as Black!** The criteria are fulfilled simply if, _by the white person's own definition_, he or she does not regard himself or herself as white! _And_, if other Black, multiracial, Asian, white Arab, mestizo, or blind people, **don't treat them as white!** (Whatever that means!) Other white people's view of them as white have no bearing on this definition at all. In fact, the definition rests only on the individual white person's *personal claim* and other desperate and confused Black people agreeing with it! It is the height of insanity!

It is the salacious attempt by Afrikans who want to include their white lovers, spouses, friends, biracial children, "Black-identified" multiracial people, and non-Afrikan sex-mates into the Afrikan group that required the writing of this treatise you have just read. This slippery slope has been left unattended for far too long of a time. It is now time for Afrikan people concerned with solving the complicated issues that Afrikan people have, and Afrikan people alone face, to stand staunchly on this **REALITY** of the true biological identity of Afrikan people as we have existed from time immemorial. We must repel the attempts by con-artists, marauders, foreigners, fakers, enemies, and fools from changing the definition of who is an Afrikan, often done to suit their own perverted sexual desires, or to try to gain power within the Afrikan collective due to the failure to do so within their own racial groups.

To continue the reclamation of our Afrikan identity, readers of this book who are in agreement with its central premise must begin to apply the concepts I have laid out in this book. In the Afrikan world, we emphatically need new and serious writers in Afrikan philosophical thought. We have to revitalize and intensify the Afrikan tradition of creating literary works. These media contents must be based on the biological reality of who is Afrikan and the Afrikan worldview. One of our tasks now is to produce prodigious material to overpower the voluminous amount of garbage being published by Afrikans with a financial hustle to practice, and to negate material by non-Afrikans who seek to engulf us with profuse amounts of fiction, theories, concepts, philosophies, tall-tales, and critiques in order to confuse, detract, and bewilder us into complacency so that we continue to follow their disastrous lead. We need to employ the scientific method to our philosophical and other works of literature so we can *constructively critique each other*, and develop our ideas intergenerationally, to arrive at the correct and thoroughly examined approaches and solutions to our problems as Afrikans. I feel that there has been a lot of focus on Kemet (ancient Egypt) to the degree that instead of fostering more understanding of our intellectual, organizational, and spiritual traditions, they have in essence spurred the creation of an Afrocentric, neo-hippie cult, that cannot really solve any problems and is still focused on "belief" rather than methodology and action. It is still focused on the veneer of Afrikanity and not the production of a tangible Afrikan world. After 40 – 100 years of reclaiming Kemet, we still do not have a large, influential, recognizably viable research institute of note, with which the best and brightest Afrikan minds seek to carry out their careers, solely dedicated to the production of theoretical knowledge and practical strategies in the interests of Afrikan people. We still do not have independent think tanks producing conceptually based policies for constructing the imminent world in which Afrikan people will thrive and direct our own future. And we definitely do not have a current leadership adopting these policy recommendations as a part of their active political agenda. Until we decide to seriously and institutionally produce and develop the minds who will help to find the solutions we need to arise out of our collective malaise, we will continue to be dominated by one or more organized power-groups who see us as their pathway to dominance, power, control, and most importantly the genetic survival of their people, at our expense.

Epilogue

by Gaspar Yanga

The African people of the world stand today at the crossroads of its existence as a people and must make a choice between two paths. The decision that African people make will decide on whether or not there will be an African people as we know it today, or as Marcus Garvey warned, Africa will be a place where in the future non-African owners of Africa will talk about a people called Negroes who once inhabited this land.

The first path is a wide path, but it is a path of momentary pleasure and temporary gains. On this path we are all inclusive, naive and gullible. Aliens are even bold enough to take our identity. As the years go by, these Aliens become more emboldened since they no longer simply want to identify as Black, they want to own and control the land of Africa, Jamaica, Haiti and the Inner Cities of Canada, US and France.

White men who seek political power no longer have to waste time in dating Black women or playing step-father to Black children, since everyone is African now, he will "just happen" to find love with a blonde-haired, blue-eyed woman in Nigeria. Since, they both can speak Yoruba and imitate African mannerisms he seeks to become President of Nigeria.

All over the new African world, Whites, Asians and Mulattoes are gaining political power. In Ghana, an African-Puerto Rican who looks like Jennifer Lopez is seeking to become the First Female Prime Minister of Ghana and her campaign is being financed by Ghanaian entrepreneur Damian Musk who plans to gain political favors once she is elected as President of Ghana.

In the United States of America, African-American civil rights icon Nkechi Amare Diallo *aka* Rachel Dolezal passes away and Bethune-Cookman University is renamed after this Black icon who suffered for the Black race. Her eulogy is read by an aging Black female icon of movies and television Cassandra Perry *aka* Tyler Perry who now identifies as a woman.

On, YouTube there is a debate about race among two Black people. Once has straight, red hair and green eyes the other has dark brown skin and African textured hair. The light skinned Black tells the dark skinned Black that the average African-American is 75% European and 25% African and that he is actually an Igbo King.

The path that we are currently on leads to no other final endgame but the complete and total extermination of the African race to be replaced as the Native-Americans were replaced by Europeans, Africans, Asians and Multi-Racial people now living on their land.

The second path is narrow path and it reads **ACBN**. This path leads to the survival and everlasting presence of Superior Saharan African people on this Earth. On this path, the Africans spirits who have been crying out from the spiritual realm finally get rest. Africans whose souls are trapped in the Indian Ocean and Atlantic Ocean are finally released from their prisons because their grandchildren have liberated themselves.

It's 2037, and CBS reports that the African Union has kicked out Morocco and has formally accepted Haiti and Jamaica to join the new Pan-African Union. The PAU announces that all Black African nations will only allow people to hold public office who have the physical traits of Africans from time immemorial.

In Atlanta, Georgia, Rachel Dolezal is assassinated by unknown assailants who can't be found. Weeks after, Shaun King was found brutally murdered in his own home. These murders are seemingly the latest in a group of murders of Whites in the United States that are unsolved.

Today in Lagos, Nigeria, *Amos N. Wilson University* announced its 10-year anniversary. Its commencement speaker will be multi-billionaire Gaspar Yanga who founded the first African-Centered Biological Nationalist University and is a Military Defense Manufacturer. Many world leaders have called Yanga a racist and a

Black supremacist, but in spite of these allegations, he remains a powerful and respected leader in Africa. His *Yanga Ballistics Corporation* is one of the largest military manufacturers in the world, employing some 50,000 Africans throughout Africa.

The United States of America seems to be on the verge of its first military defense since Vietnam as many South Koreans have begun to defect and fight with North Korea in the Anglo-American-Korean War. Many, Americans are calling for a world embargo on Yanga Ballistics for arming the North Koreans with the latest in African technology which the Americans thought would not be effective.

The Pew Research Center claims that there is a global marriage rush among Black couples. Many sociologists and researchers are alarmed at the large number of opposite sex couples that are exploding throughout the Black world stating that in 100 years there could be 3 billion African people walking the face of the planet with a world that is allegedly already over populated.

Those of you who are willing to take the ACBN path will work to establish the founding of a Biological Nationalist empire whose only natural, spiritual and political limits shall be the *galaxies and our imaginations* which will know no bounds and shall remember AFRICAN FIRST…at home and abroad.

Abibifawhodie!

Endnotes

Chapter 1

1. Definition take from Bhekizitha author and founder of acbnj.wordpress.com
2. See the following articles, "Richa Adhia". Accessed at https://en.wikipedia.org/wiki/Richa_Adhia. Oct 2016. "Syrian, Lebanese represent Venezuela, Tanzania in Miss Universe, 2016". Accessed at http://english.alarabiya.net/en/life-style/entertainment/2017/01/29/Syrian-and-Lebanese-contestants-represent-Venezuela-Tanzania-in-Miss-Universe-2017.html, *and* Mixed-race individuals have also been winners of the contest. See the following, "Lisa Jensen". Accessed at http://www.universalqueen.com/2012/07/lisa-jensen-tanzania-miss-world-2012.html, http://www.bongocinema.com/casts/view/lisa-jensen, *and* "Angela Damas". Accessed at http://www.missiepopular.com/2013/07/throwback-thursday-angela-damasmiss.html. The purpose of this exposé is not to lambast multiracial people, but to bring attention to the sly way in which the Afrikan identity is being manipulated to include non-Afrikans under the faux rationale of passport nationalism and accentuating non-Afrikan beauty standards through "official" and "impartial" contests.
3. Jaramillo, C. (May 2017). " 'Not black enough?' Biracial winner of Miss Black University of Texas draws backlash". Dallas News. Accessed at https://www.dallasnews.com/life/life/2017/05/03/miss-black-university-texas-gets-internet-backlash-black-enough.
4. See, "The African Diaspora in the Indian Ocean" particularly the section on Ethiopia. Accessed at http://exhibitions.nypl.org/africansindianocean/essay-east-africa.php. June, 2017
5. From the film, "Annie Hall". Written by Woody Allen and Marshall Brickman. Metro-Goldwyn-Mayer. 1977
6. CIA Factbook. Accessed at https://www.cia.gov/library/publications/the-world-factbook/fields/2075.html. June, 2017.
7. Esseissah, K. (2016). "Paradise Is Under the Feet of Your Master" The Construction of the Religious Basis of Racial Slavery in the Mauritanian Arab-Berber Community. *Journal of Black Studies*, *47*(1), 3-23.
8. CIA Factbook, Ibid.
9. United Nations Economic Commission for Africa, *The Demographic Profile of African Countries* p. 26. (Addis Ababa: United Nations, 2015). Accessed at http://www.uneca.org/sites/default/files/PublicationFiles/demographic_profile_rev_april_25.pdf.

10. The *Afrikan Sovereignty Project* is the movement focused on gaining true and lasting sovereignty for Afrikan people, particularly those Afrikans in the diaspora who are descendants of the victims of *The Black Chattelization War, 1442-1888*

11. Njinga, Seestah Imukhus. (2009) *Ababio: A 21st venture anthology of African diasporan returnees to Ghana.* (p.124). Accra, Ghana: One Africa Tours and Specialty Services Ltd.

12. Strober, R. (2015) *Hottest dark.* LNR Enterprises, INC.

13. Wright, B.E. (1979) *Mentacide: The ultimate threat to the Black race.* Publisher unknown. Retrieved at https://sankoreconnect.files.wordpress.com/2011/01/mentacide-the-ultimate-threat-to-the-black-race.pdf.

14. The author of this text does not reject the theory of evolution outright, but recognizes that some holes still exist in its explanation and the "official" interpretation of facts. Furthermore, the theory has been (mis)applied for political ends. For more explanation of the gaps and political application of the theory. See the article; Jones, F. (2015) "*White People Did Not Originate in Africa*". Accessed at https://amosmagazine.wordpress.com/2017/06/15/white-people-did-not-originate-in-africa-by-f-jones/.

15a. Umoja, & Pam, T. (2011) *Black love is a revolutionary act.* Chicago: Trojan Horse Press.

15b. Umoja, & Pam, T. (2011) *The interracial con game.* Chicago: Trojan Horse Press.

16. The "*one-drop*" rule or the hypodescent rule indicates that if a person has **ANY** Afrikan ancestry, noticeable or not, then one is designated as "Black", or more correctly "*Negro*", in the parlance of the time. Although this rule existed in social terms prior, the US Supreme Court's decision in the case of "Plessy v. Ferguson" (1896) ensconced this social practice into law in which it was determined that a mixed-race individual (Plessy) could not use the railcar reserved for whites on a train. This reinforced the decision by Chief Justice Roger Taney in the "Dred Scott Case" (1857) who opined that, "No negro had any rights that white men are bound to respect". This meant that the hypodescent rule extended the practice of segregation to Afrikan and non-Afrikans alike by creating a class of fully Afrikan and mixed-race individuals in US law called the "Negro". However, this legal decision had no basis in biological or genetic research or fact. See the article; Maddox, A. (Feb 2016). "Nominating a Black Nationalist". Accessed at http://universityofaltonmaddox.com/site/nominating-a-black-nationalist/.

17. "Mixed-racism" is the author's term and is defined as the practice of people who hate and are hostile to those who do not openly and with reverence accept the racial treason of a person's decision to organize one's life to

specifically produce mixed-race people because of their personal psychological issues associated with being a member of one's own race.

18. From the film, "Deconstructing Harry". Written by Woody Allen. Sweetland Films & Jean Doumanian Productions. 1997.

Chapter 2

1. Umoja, & Pam, T. (2011) *The interracial con game.* Chicago: Trojan Horse Press.

2. Fanon, F. (1952). *Black skin, white masks.* London: Pluto Press.

3. Umoja, & Pam, T. (2012) *The beauty con game.* Chicago: Trojan Horse Press

4. Baruti, Mwalimu K. B. (2000). *Excuses, excuses.* Atlanta: Akoben House.

5. Wilson, A. (1993). *The falsification of Afrikan consciousness.* New York: Afrikan World InfoSystems.

6. Discussion in video entitled "Interracial Relationships are Destructive to the Black Afrikan Family". Accessed at https://youtu.be/r-RDbRau2i8. March 2017

7. Asimov, I. (2010). *The foundation trilogy.* London: Knopf. The concept of "psychohistory" started as a plot device in the science fiction work of Isaac Asimov. It is defined in his book as "a blend of crowd psychology and high-level math…it is a new field of science that equates all possibilities in large societies to mathematics, allowing for the prediction of future events." Quote taken from, Durden, T. (2017). "Foundation – Fall of the American Galactic Empire". Accessed at http://www.zerohedge.com/news/2017-03-27/foundation-fall-american-galactic-empire. Much like the forerunner to the cell phone or smart phone can be seen in science fiction works like *Star Trek*, this concept of *psychohistory* too has beginnings in the literary imagination which has since been applied to the study of social sciences. The use of the concept of *psychohistory* does not indicate some reliance on mysticism by the author, but the concept is used as a tool to relate the broader argument of this book to the reader for clearer understanding. *Psychohistory* is also defined as "the science of historical motivations, (and) combines the insights of psychotherapy with the research methodology of the social sciences to understand the emotional origin of the social and political behavior of groups and nations, past and present." From, psychohistory.com.

8. Willis, K. (May 2017). "Ex-WWE Star Ariane Andrew Explains Why She Doesn't Date Black Guys". Atlanta Black Star article. Retrieved from https://www.abibitumikasa.com/forums/showthread.php?t=211784

9. I reject the term white "supremacy" because whites are NOT supreme. The term I prefer and think is more accurate for their sociopolitical-economic system is *white hegemony.* Meaning whites and people defined as white, feel they have the right to infiltrate any and every plane of existence and

attempt to define, direct, manage, own, and control it at the expense of the non-white, and particularly Afrikans.

10. Ani, Marimba. (1994) *Yurugu: An Afrikan-centered critique of European cultural thought and behavior.* Washington D.C.: Nkonimfo Publications. This text explains more in depth this inherent European behavior.

11. Quote take from video lecture, "Stolen Property-The Spiritman: Dr. Amos Wilson Black Dollers" (sic). Video accessed at https://youtu.be/qMs_qMDBYLM. Oct 2012.

12. Moore, T., Hensley, N., & Siemaszko, C. (2015). "Deputy involved in body-slam arrest of Spring Valley High student is dating a black woman, so he can't be racist, sheriff says". Daily News. Accessed at http://www.nydailynews.com/news/national/spring-valley-high-school-officer-tackled-teen-phone-article-1.2412665.

13. See the discussion in *Yurugu*, by Dr. Marimba Ani.

14. Bibliography of Dr. Wilson, the Ideological father of ACBN:
Black on Black Violence (1990)
The Developmental Psychology of the Black Child (1978)
Awakening the Natural Genius of Black Children (1992)
Afrikan-Centered Consciousness versus the New World Order (1990)
Blueprint for Black Power (1998)
Understanding Black Adolescent Male Violence (1992)
The Falsification of Afrikan Consciousness (1993)

15. Chinweizu, I. (1987). *Decolonising the African mind.* SUNDOOR.

16. Wilson, A. (1990). *Black on Black violence. The psychodynamics of Black self-annihilation in service of white domination.* New York: Afrikan World InfoSystems.

17. Kambon. K. (1992). *The Afrikan personality in America: An Afrikan-Centered Framework.* Nubian Nation Publications.

18. All articles reprinted with permission from the author of The Lumumba Afrika Report. Accessed at lumumbaafrika.wordpress.com

19. Quote from Martin Luther King's, "I Have a Dream" speech given at the March on Washington, 1963

20. See note 18

21. Ibid.

Chapter 3

1. RBG Street Scholar. (2009). "Dr. Bobby E. Wright on Proper Student Education, the Psychopathic Racial Personality, and more". Accessed at https://rbgstreetscholar.wordpress.com/2009/08/16/dr-bobby-e-wright-on-proper-black-student-education-the-psychopathic-racial-personality-and-more-2/.

2. Quote from the video of the talk "Blueprint for Black Power". Accessed at https://youtu.be/hKkGfJV4ZWk. June 2016.

3. Muhammad, E. (1965). *Message to the Black man.* Phoenix: Secretarius MEMPS Publications.

4. Makesi-Tehuti, K. (2006). *How to make a negro Christian.* Bolekaja Enterprises.

5. Williams, W. (1998). *The historical origin of Christianity*, and; *The historical origins of Islam.* (2003). Chicago: Maathian Press, Inc.

6. Definition taken from the online journal African Centered Biological Journal retrieved from www.acbnj.wordpress.com on January 17, 2016.

7. These begin my additions to the definition.

8. *Nguzo Saba* means *"Seven Principles"* in Kiswahili. These are principles associated with the Afrikan-American created holiday known as Kwanzaa. They are:

   - Umoja (Unity)
   - Kujichagulia (Self-Determination)
   - Ujima (Work & Responsibility)
   - Ujamaa (Cooperative Economics)
   - Nia (Purpose)
   - Kuumba (Creativity)
   - Imani (Faith)

   Although ACBN does not specifically endorse nor reject Kwanzaa, the Nguzo Saba are solid foundations for organization and activity which can be an integral part of any ACBN institution. See, officialkwanzaawebsite.org for more information.

9. The amount of work is wide and varied however, one can begin by examining the work of Dr. Josef Ben Jochannan, Odwirafo, K. Kia Bunseki Fu-Kiau, and Dr. Obadele Kambon in his online video series called *"The Foundations of Afrikan Thought"* available at abibitumikasa.com

Chapter 4

1. Griffin, G.E. (1994). *Creature from Jekyll Island.* California: American Media.

2. Durden, Tyler. (2017). "Opioids Killed More People in One Ohio County Last Year Than Car Accidents, Homicides, & Suicides Combined". Zero Hedge. Accessed at http://www.zerohedge.com/news/2017-06-12/opioids-killed-more-people-one-ohio-country-last-year-car-accidents-homicides-and-su. June 2017.

3. Bureau of Labor Statistics. "Labor Force Statistics from the Current Population Survey". (2017). US Department of Labor. Accessed at https://www.bls.gov/cps/cpsaat05.htm, and Bureau of Labor Statistics. "Labor Force Statistics from the Current Population Survey". (2017). Bureau of Labor Statistics. US Department of Labor. Accessed at https://www.bls.gov/cps/cpsaat18.htm, and BLS Reports. "Labor force characteristics by race and ethnicity, 2015". US Department of Labor.

Accessed at https://www.bls.gov/opub/reports/race-and-ethnicity/2015/home.htm. See also, Thompson, D. (2013). "The Workforce is Even More Divided by Race Than You Think". The Atlantic. Accessed at https://www.theatlantic.com/business/archive/2013/11/the-workforce-is-even-more-divided-by-race-than-you-think/281175/.

4. Wood, P. (2015). *Technocracy Rising: The Trojan Horse of Global Transformation.* USA: Coherent Publishing.

5. Lundberg, F. (1937). *America's 60 Families.* New York: Vanguard Press, and; Gilens, M., & Page, B. I. (2014). Testing theories of American politics: Elites, interest groups, and average citizens. *Perspectives on politics, 12*(03), 564-581. Retrieved from https://scholar.princeton.edu/sites/default/files/mgilens/files/gilens_and_page_2014_-testing_theories_of_american_politics.doc.pdf.

6. Griffin, G.E., *Creature from Jekyll Island.*

7. Chinweizu, I. (2010) *Pan Africanism and a Black superpower—the 21st century agenda.* Accra: Paper submitted to the CBAAC conference on Pan-Africanism. Abuja. Accessed at http://houseofknowledge.org.uk/newsite/index.php/written-resources/chinweizu-corner.

8. Wilson, A. (1998). *Blueprint for Black Power.* New York. Afrikan World InfoSystems.

9. Ani, Marimba. (1994) *Yurugu: An Afrikan-centered critique of European cultural thought and behavior.* Washington D.C.: Nkonimfo Publications.

10. Ackerman, E. (1997). "His Music Rules Haiti". Miami New Times. Accessed at http://www.miaminewtimes.com/news/his-music-rules-in-haiti-6360759. Also see, Danto, E. (2011). "Martelly: Haiti's Second Great Disaster", and Danto, E. (2015). "US Election Scams in Haiti". Accessed at http://www.ezilidanto.com/.

11. Pendleton, T. (2017). "Shea Moisture Pulls Ad After Online Backlash". Black America Web. Accessed at https://blackamericaweb.com/2017/04/25/shea-moisture-pulls-ad-after-online-backlash/, and Reid, J. (2017). "Inside Her Story: SheaMositure CEO on Controversial Commercial: 'It Was A Mistake'". Black America Web. Accessed at https://blackamericaweb.com/2017/04/28/inside-her-story-sheamoisture-ceo-on-controversial-commercial-it-was-a-mistake/.

12. See these various articles: *Kit Carson.* Accessed at https://www.biography.com/people/kit-carson-9239728. Encyclopedia of World Biography. *Kit Carson Biography.* Accessed at http://www.notablebiographies.com/Ca-Ch/Carson-Kit.html. Wikipedia. *Kit Carson.* https://en.wikipedia.org/wiki/Kit_Carson. Also see, Carson, Kit. *Kit Carson's Autobiography.* Edited by Milo Milton Quaife. Chicago: R. R. Donnelley & Sons Co., 1935. Reprint, Lincoln: University of Nebraska Press, 1966.

13. Sawe, B.E. (2017). "African Countries By Population Density". World Facts: WorldAtlas.com. Accessed at http://www.worldatlas.com/articles/african-countries-by-population-density.html. Also see, Population Density. (2017). Accessed at https://en.wikipedia.org/wiki/Population_density, *and* United Nations Economic Commission for Africa, *The Demographic Profile of African Countries* pp. 7-8. (Addis Ababa: United Nations, 2015). Accessed at http://www.uneca.org/sites/default/files/PublicationFiles/demographic_profile_rev_april_25.pdf.
14. Chinweizu, I. (2010). *Afrocentric Rectification of Terms 5*. Received through personal correspondence with the author.
15. Kambon, O. (2016). "Knowledge Production And Its Associated Cottage Industries". Black Star News. Accessed at http://www.blackstarnews.com/global-politics/africa/knowledge-production-and-its-associated-cottage-industries. Also see the video lecture, "Make Afrika Great Again! Divest from America – Invest in Afrika". Accessed at https://abibitumikasa.com/forums/showthread.php/193421-Divest-from-America-Invest-in-Africa-Knowledge-Production-and-its-Associated-Cottage-Industries.

Chapter 5
1. See, "Black Afrikan Infrastructure Organization (BAIO)". Accessed at http://baioafrikstan5.ning.com/main/authorization/signUp?. Also, "Mr. Holipsism". Website address at holipsism.com/.
2. Baruti, Mwalimu K. B. (2014). *Message to the warriors.* Atlanta: Akoben House.
3. Quoted in a discussion on "Afrika Speaks – with Alkebu-lan". June 2017. Accessed at https://youtu.be/Vm6VcSSXr_o. Also see, "Aims and Objectives of Momentum Black Connexions". Accessed at https://momentumblackconnexions.wordpress.com/2016/05/01/aims-and-objectives-of-momentum-black-connexions/.
4. Warren, L. (2015). "Rachel Dolezal the NAACP Leader Outed as WHITE by Her Parents". Mail Online. Accessed at http://www.dailymail.co.uk/news/article-3121061/Local-NAACP-leader-professor-African-studies-outed-WHITE-parents-convincing-community-black-years.html.
5. LaCapria, K. (2015). Shaun King Racial Controversy". Snopes. Updated Jan 2016. Accessed at http://www.snopes.com/2015/08/19/shaun-king/.

Photo Credits
(*Listed in the order depicted*)

Image Source: (Afrikans in the coffle lines) From the article, (2015). "The Transatlantic Slave trade – 16-19th Century". Devastating Disasters. Accessed at https://devastatingdisasters.com/the-transatlantic-slave-trade-16-19th-century/.

Image Source: (Afrikans handcuffed on the ship) From the article, J.L.H.D. (2012). "Legacy of Distrust". The Economist: Atlanta. Accessed at http://www.economist.com/whichmba/legacy-distrust.

Image Source: (HMS Daphne) From the online forum, (2015). "Photos of 19th Century Arab Slave Trade of East Africans". The Coli. Accessed at http://www.thecoli.com/threads/photos-of-19th-century-arab-slave-trade-of-east-africans.297388/. Information on the HMS Daphne from, https://en.wikipedia.org/wiki/HMS_Daphne_(1866)

Image Source: (Afrikans and Arabs) Arab Slave Trade, (2017). "19th-century engraving of Arab slave-trading caravan transporting African slaves across the Sahara". Accessed at https://en.wikipedia.org/wiki/Arab_slave_trade.

Image Source of next three photos: (Afrikan boys; On the ship; Afrikan woman) From the online forum, (2015). "Photos of 19th Century Arab Slave Trade of East Africans". The Coli. Accessed at http://www.thecoli.com/threads/photos-of-19th-century-arab-slave-trade-of-east-africans.297388/.

Image Source: Ilhan Omar taken from http://www.startribune.com/ilhan-omar-will-be-nation-s-first-somali-american-legislator/400478961/.

Image Source: Somali President Hassan Sheikh Mohamud taken from http://www.bbc.com/news/world-africa-34465949

Image Source: Somalis, some with Afrikan features some without. Taken from https://www.somalispot.com/threads/what-is-your-skin-tone.27330/page-6.

Image Source: Ethiopian mixed woman. Image credit: Harvey Sapir Photography Pikiwiki Israel. Taken from http://traumaweb.org/ethiopian-community/.

Image Source: Ethiopian man Tedros Adhanom Ghebreyesus taken from http://edition.cnn.com/2017/05/24/health/who-appoints-first-african-dg/index.html.

Image Source: (Afrikan women and children) "19th century slave portraits". Accessed at https://es.pinterest.com/pin/28921622582767207/.

Image Source: (Men and boys on the dock) From article, "Not just a number anymore: Website traces the African slaves who shaped America by name and

country of origin". (2011). Mail Online. Accessed at
http://www.dailymail.co.uk/news/article-1391155/Not-just-number--Website-trace-African-slaves-shaped-America-country-origin.html.

Image Source: (Young Afrikan girl) "19th century slave portraits". Accessed at
https://es.pinterest.com/pin/28921622582767217/.

Image Source: (Afrikan woman with hand to her face) "19th century slave portraits".
Accessed at https://es.pinterest.com/pin/28921622582767186/.

Image Source: (Five Afrikan woman and girl) Library of Congress Prints and
Photographs Division. "Ruins of Richmond & Petersburg railroad bridge from
island in James River," Reproduction Number: LC-DIG-cwpb-00388, Call
Number: LC-B815- 846. Accessed at
https://jubiloemancipationcentury.wordpress.com/category/women/.

Image Source: (Afrikan caregiver) "19th century slave portraits". Accessed at
https://es.pinterest.com/pin/462956036674588792/.

Image Source: (Mulatto with fan) Photograph courtesy Louisiana State University
Libraries, Thomas H. and Joan W. Gandy Photograph Collection, Item Number
37780413103a. Accessed at
https://jubiloemancipationcentury.wordpress.com/2015/08/20/portaits-from-natchez-mississippi/.

Image Source: (Seated Mulatto writer) Political Hotwire. (2016). Thread, "19th
Century Black Literature". Accessed at http://politicalhotwire.com/world-history/147259-19th-century-black-literature.html.

Image Source: (Mulatto child) Photograph courtesy Louisiana State University
Libraries, Thomas H. and Joan W. Gandy Photograph Collection, Item Number
37780413114a. Accessed at
https://jubiloemancipationcentury.wordpress.com/2015/08/20/portaits-from-natchez-mississippi/.

Image Source: (Mixed-race girl with fan) Photograph courtesy Louisiana State
University Libraries, Thomas H. and Joan W. Gandy Photograph Collection, Item
Number 37780413109a. Accessed at
https://jubiloemancipationcentury.wordpress.com/2015/08/20/portaits-from-natchez-mississippi/.

Image Source: (Daniel Payne) From the article, "Daniel Payne" (2017). Wikipedia.
Accessed at https://en.wikipedia.org/wiki/Daniel_Payne.

Image Source: (William Wells Brown) From the article, "William Wells Brown"
(2017). Wikipedia. Accessed at
https://en.wikipedia.org/wiki/William_Wells_Brown.

Image Source: (Frederick Douglass) From the article, "Former slave and leading abolitionist Frederick Douglass revealed to be the most photographed American of the 19th century". (2015). Mail Online. Accessed at http://www.dailymail.co.uk/news/article-3282040/Former-slave-leading-abolitionist-Frederick-Douglass-revealed-photographed-American-19th-century.html.

Image Source: (Negro Soldier) https://es.pinterest.com/pin/230879918370453499/.

Image Source: (Rhineland Bastard) https://es.pinterest.com/pin/155937205819278887/.

Image Source: (Afrikan mother and daughter) https://es.pinterest.com/pin/408842472393130483/.

Image Source: ("Light-skinned" slave & negro husband) "Jubilo! The Emancipation Century: African Americans in the 19th Century: Slavery, Resistance, Abolition, the Civil War, Emancipation, Reconstruction, and the Nadir". Accessed at https://jubiloemancipationcentury.wordpress.com/category/women/.

About the Author

Kwesi Anan Ababio.

Kwesi Anan Ababio trained in biology and linguistics in both America and Asia. He has had a multi-faceted career in health, recreation, education, writing, and entertainment. This eclectic experience is what informs his writing on politics and social philosophy in the present publication. Currently, he enjoys spending quiet time at home with his family. He can be contacted via email for queries concerning this publication.

email: herunefer@gmail.com

www.ingramcontent.com/pod-product-compliance
Lightning Source LLC
Chambersburg PA
CBHW031515270326
41930CB00006B/410